At Issue

| Urban Farming

Other Books in the At Issue Series:

At Issue

Urban Farming

Tamara Thompson, Book Editor

GREENHAVEN PRESS
A part of Gale, Cengage Learning

GALE
CENGAGE Learning·

Farmington Hills, Mich • San Francisco • New York • Waterville, Maine
Meriden, Conn • Mason, Ohio • Chicago

Elizabeth Des Chenes, *Director, Content Strategy*
Douglas Dentino, *Manager, New Product*

© 2014 Greenhaven Press, a part of Gale, Cengage Learning

WCN: 01-100-101

For more information, contact:
Greenhaven Press
27500 Drake Rd.
Farmington Hills, MI 48331-3535
Or you can visit our Internet site at gale.cengage.com

For product information and technology assistance, contact us at

Gale Customer Support, 1-800-877-4253
For permission to use material from this text or product, submit all requests online at www.cengage.com/permissions

Further permissions questions can be emailed to permissionrequest@cengage.com

Articles in Greenhaven Press anthologies are often edited for length to meet page requirements. In addition, original titles of these works are changed to clearly present the main thesis and to explicitly indicate the author's opinion. Every effort is made to ensure that Greenhaven Press accurately reflects the original intent of the authors. Every effort has been made to trace the owners of copyrighted material.

Cover image © Images.com/Corbis.

LIBRARY OF CONGRESS CATALOGING-IN-PUBLICATION DATA

Urban farming / Tamara Thompson, book editor.
    pages cm. -- (At issue)
Includes bibliographical references and index.
ISBN 978-0-7377-6868-8 (hardcover) -- ISBN 978-0-7377-6869-5 (pbk.)
1. Urban agriculture. 2. Land use, Urban. 3. Urban livestock production systems.
I. Thompson, Tamara, editor of compilation.
S494.5.U72U76 2014
635.09173'2--dc23
                                                    2014001102

Printed in the United States of America
1 2 3 4 5 6 7 18 17 16 15 14

Contents

Introduction

When most folks think of farms, they think of the country, not the city. But people have been successfully growing food and raising animals in urban areas for centuries. Paris, for example, has a long tradition of intensive urban agriculture dating back to the 1800s, and Havana, Cuba, currently grows some 90 percent of its fresh produce within city limits. In the United States, a new wave of interest in eating locally grown food and achieving self-sufficiency has developed into a bona fide urban agriculture movement over the past decade. What started out as a trend for backyard hobbyists and self-proclaimed urban homesteaders has since grown into a mainstream phenomenon; even the White House now has an organic vegetable garden and beehives.

Urban farming can take many forms: a few tomato plants on an apartment balcony; vacant lots cultivated by neighbors; formally structured school or community garden programs; illegal guerrilla gardening in public spaces; nonprofit, educational, or for-profit urban farms (sometimes on rooftops!); backyard bees, chickens, and other small animals kept for their eggs, meat, milk, and honey; and much more.

What all these things have in common, though, is "an intentional effort by an individual or community to grow its capacity for self-sufficiency and well-being through the cultivation of plants and animals," according to Edwin Marty, coauthor of *Breaking Through Concrete: Building an Urban Farm Revival*.

There are just as many motivations for urban farming as there are ways of doing it: addressing inner-city "food deserts" where fresh produce is unavailable; getting closer to one's food by practicing local and organic eating; increasing sustainability and reducing the carbon footprint of food by reducing the miles it must travel before it is consumed; increasing a community's food security by improving self-sufficiency and resilience to disaster; boosting local economies and creating jobs; reducing family food budgets and improving public health; strengthening community relationships; reclaiming and revitalizing neglected inner-city spaces; preserving immigrants' cultural food traditions; and providing job training and rehabilitation, to name a few.

For these reasons and more, cities nationwide have begun investing in a variety of urban agriculture projects, and others are changing their municipal codes to allow previously banned small-scale urban farming activities, such as keeping chickens or selling homegrown vegetables. In 2013, California passed legislation to encourage community gardens and small farms in urban areas by allowing cities to lower the assessed value and property taxes on properties three acres or smaller if owners promise to grow food on them for at least five years. New York City recently invested $600,000 to help expand a rooftop farm, which grows more than forty thousand pounds of organic produce for local consumption each year. Seattle is developing a seven-acre public "food forest" in the middle of the city, planted with fruit and nut trees as well as herbs and vegetables. And economically devastated Detroit—mired in an $18 billion bankruptcy filing and saddled with an estimated one hundred and fifty thousand vacant and abandoned properties—recently revised its municipal code to attract urban agriculture projects in the hopes of cleaning up urban blight, creating jobs, and revitalizing the city.

But not everyone thinks urban farming is a great idea. For every story about a city embracing the urban farming ethos, there is another in which a municipality has punished residents for their back-to-the-land activities. In the past year, for example, officials in several cities around the country ordered residents to remove their front-yard vegetable gardens or face stiff daily fines, and a town in Pennsylvania used revised zoning laws to force a family to get rid of its chickens, dairy goats, and a small tractor, which they'd used on their three-acre property since 1976.

Despite a general trend toward permitting more urban farming activities, rather than less, urban agriculture restrictions of one sort or other remain common in cities from coast to coast. Many cities prohibit residents from keeping bees, chickens, or other farm animals, or they place restrictions on the types of plants that may be grown on a property or the kinds of things that can take place there.

Critics often maintain that urban farming activities detract from residential property values and that they emit unpleasant odors and noises, attract rodents, increase the prevalence of animal cruelty, and present public health risks. Especially controversial is the backyard slaughter of chickens and other small animals. Most cities that permit small farm animals in urban areas still prohibit their on-site slaughter, but others, such as Oakland, California, are considering clear guidelines to regulate the practice because they acknowledge that it goes on anyway.

While many people say backyard husbandry is simply a natural outgrowth of the urban farming movement, others believe that it undermines urban agriculture as a whole because it shifts the focus away from plants and creates unwelcome controversy. The authors in At Issue: Urban Farming examine these and other issues related to the increasingly popular practice of growing food and keeping farm animals in urban areas.

1

Overview: The Urban Farming Movement

Edwin Marty

Edwin Marty is the founder of the nonprofit Jones Valley Urban Farm in downtown Birmingham, Alabama, and the coauthor, with David Hanson, of Breaking Through Concrete: Building an Urban Farm Revival, *from which the following viewpoint is taken. Marty is also the executive director of the Hampstead Institute, a nonprofit farm in downtown Montgomery, Alabama, that offers community planting beds, you-pick fruits, an orchard, and learning opportunities with a farmer-in-residence.*

Although there have always been some folks who raise fruits and vegetables in cities, over the last decade there has been an explosion in interest in urban farming, with hundreds of significant projects sprouting up nationwide. There are many different types of models that fall under the urban farming rubric—small farms that are either nonprofit or for-profit ventures, community gardens, and school gardens to name just a few. Participants come from all walks of life, but they all share the common goal of increasing self-reliance and furthering sustainability. Urban farms increase access to fresh produce for better public health, improve food security, reduce dependence on fossil fuels, boost local economies, and help build strong communities.

I've spent the last ten years developing Jones Valley Urban Farm into a thriving nonprofit, with over twenty-eight acres that produce healthy food and provide educational programs to thousands of youths and adults throughout the city. The farm's vision has evolved from focusing primarily on transforming vacant lots into productive farms to contributing to the slow but steady progression toward a more sustainable food system, a return to a consciousness about health and food and community.

Not surprisingly, I've found that the things that motivated me to commit my life to farming in the city were not unique. A dedicated core of urban farm entrepreneurs has emerged among my generation that sits somewhere between the hippies of the 1960s and Generation Y. Jones Valley Urban Farm is just one of the hundreds of projects started in the last decade that are responding to the opportunities in modern American cities. While good urban planning promotes dense land use, it is rarely achieved, and over time a waning of intensity inevitably sets in. It is nearly impossible for planners to create a contingency plan for what will happen if a strip mall fails, a new interstate project cuts off a community, or a housing development isn't fully occupied. In the past, kudzu in the South, blackberries in Seattle, or garlic mustard in Detroit filled this void.

A Radical Shift

But early in this century, farmers across the United States radically shifted the battle lines of urban development and urban decay. No longer are invasive species given a decade's head start. Coupled with a significant resurgence of interest in local food, farmers are staking claim to open urban space and finding fertile ground beneath the canopy of neglect. Although urban farming is far from a new endeavor (the Persians were composting urban waste in 1000 B.C.E.), a significant boom in interest has occurred around the country in the last decade, and it has a broad and varied community. Unlike previous waves of interest in urban farming, the blossoming of projects in the twenty-first century cuts cleanly across racial and demographic profiles. Cities such as Detroit have been experimenting with urban farm projects for well over a hundred years. But the previous attempts were usually government-funded endeavors intended to "dig" out of a recession or provide stimulus to the local economy through job creation.

Perhaps the only "concrete" theme that draws all of these projects and people together is their intention.

The latest wave of urban farming is harder to classify. Community gardens with roots dating back decades are still thriving in cities like New York and Seattle. School gardens are being linked with hands-on science classes and changing what's served in the cafeterias. For-profit farms are taking advantage of a trend toward purchasing locally produced food at farmer's markets. And still more nonprofit urban farms are providing job training and social services. . . .

Who are these people changing the look of urban communities and what are their motives? Are they acting in isolation or are they part of a larger shift in consciousness throughout the country?

What Is an Urban Farm?

During talks and lectures about Jones Valley Urban Farm, I find myself regularly answering the question, what is an urban farm? While on one level it seems quite obvious—farming in a city—finding a workable definition is more difficult. Are community gardeners who don't sell their produce farmers? When does a city end and a suburb begin? Does growing landscape plants for sale constitute urban farming? If so, is every Home Depot and Lowe's actually an urban farm?

To answer these questions, we asked many of the farmers, gardeners, and community supporters from around the country how they would define urban farming. The answers were as diverse as the projects we profiled. Some considered urban farms places where communities take back their autonomy. Others focused on income generation. Still others concentrated on education. Perhaps the only "concrete" theme that draws all of these projects and people together is their *intention*. Everyone is striving to create a healthier community where people know their neighbors and have access to good food. I've pulled all these threads together and propose this working definition of urban farming: *An urban farm is an intentional effort by an individual or a community to grow its capacity for self-sufficiency and well-being through the cultivation of plants and/or animals.*

Building on this broad definition of urban farming, we can divide the projects ... into three simple categories.

URBAN FARMS: Either for-profit or nonprofit organizations that are growing produce, flowers, herbs, and/or animals within a city. These organizations have a paid staff that produces products for sale for a local market only.

COMMUNITY GARDENS: An individual or collection of individuals growing plants and/or animals on either public property or private property for their own consumption or to donate to the needy.

The urban farm is an ideal platform for generating dialogue among various parts of a community.

SCHOOL GARDENS: A garden located on a school campus that acts as a laboratory in conjunction with an academic class, a demonstration, or a source of food for the students. Farm to School programs, which link local farmers with school cafeterias and provide education to students, often work closely with school gardens to increase the consumption of local, fresh produce by students and school staff.

Toward a Sustainable System

It is generally recognized that urban farms will never have the capacity to feed the entire population, although cities such as Havana, Cuba, are purportedly capable of supplying most of the fresh vegetables for the city's needs. Urban farms can, however, fill an important role in a broader effort to create a more sustainable and just food system. Phrases such as *agricultural urbanism* and *community food security* point to an intricate web of rural and urban farmers connected directly to local consumers and supported by government policy.... Urban farming is a critical player in the development of the future food system, not only in terms of production, but also, and more profoundly, in terms of advocacy and education.

The most important role of the urban farm is perhaps in the physical manifestation of the vision for a truly sustainable food system, and in the bringing together of the people who can make that happen. The urban farm is an ideal platform for generating dialogue among various parts of a community. Children learn what local fresh food tastes like and develop a desire for more. College students study the systems that control our food supply and get to put theory into practice by working on an urban farm. Parents have a place to purchase high-quality fresh, local food and see what a community could look like if it supported more local agriculture. Legislators witness a vivid example of good policy—community gardens thriving on every corner—as opposed to the end result of bad policy—more "food deserts" full of abandoned strip malls and unhealthy citizens without access to fresh food.

"Eat Your View" is a popular slogan in Europe. The idea is simple. When you buy food, you are voting. You are voting in favor of the way your purchase was produced, processed, distributed, and marketed. When you buy food from a local urban farm, you are increasing the demand for more local urban farms. Buy enough food and you will eventually be surrounded by farms. That means that urban farms are essentially the manifestation of consumers' desires to see a more just and sustainable food system—and to eat good food.

Why Are Urban Farms Appearing Right Now?

While there are thousands of different reasons to start an urban farm, a couple of themes seem to recur. . . . Urban farms create a country that is less dependent on nonrenewable fossil fuels and has healthier citizens eating better food, communities with stronger economies and more jobs, and cities that provide their youth inspiration rather than desperation.

But why is all this happening right now? Perhaps the most significant shift that has occurred to create a fertile ground for urban farming is the view that cities should not be mindlessly consuming products made outside their borders, that they could be at least partially self-sufficient.

There is a growing recognition that our nation's public health is in peril due to what we are eating.

In her book *City Bountiful*, Laura Lawson has carefully documented the waves of interest in urban farming that have washed over America during the last century. These booms have usually accompanied significant financial stress or war. Municipalities and individuals have found urban farming to be both effective and affirming. Although it is possible that we are experiencing just another one of the booms Lawson cites, the diversity of projects currently thriving across the country points to deeper roots and perhaps a profound transformation in the way America views urban development and food systems.

The last decade has seen a huge increase in interest in local food, from celebrity chefs touting their fresh products to farmer's markets popping up around cities faster than mushrooms after a rain. Urban farms have obviously benefited di-

rectly from this interest. There is no better way to get fresh local food than from a farm down the street. But is this just a
fad? Perhaps if this were occurring in isolation, the longevity
of the interest could be expected to fade quickly. However, a
couple of other trends are building that promise to change the
foundation of our communities before this boom dissipates.

Public Health and Economics

There is a growing recognition that our nation's public health
is in peril due to what we are eating. The number of studies
linking obesity and chronic disease to our diet expands expo-
nentially each year. A consensus finally exists that public health
advocates have to do more than address food-safety issues.
What we are eating must change or we as a country will face
significant negative impacts on our economy and even national security. With this understanding, there is little dis-
agreement that increasing consumption of fresh fruits and
vegetables is a simple solution, especially among children. Urban farms respond to this need perfectly.

Having children participate in the production of what
they eat is a well-tested method for increasing their lifelong
consumption of healthy foods. The idea is simple. If a child
helps to grow something, he or she is more likely to experiment with that food. Once a child has eaten a certain food, he
or she is more likely to try it again. And from there it's a small
step to achieving a long-standing behavioral change—a change
that began with putting a seed in the ground. So with the
country's population steadily shifting to urban living, urban
farms are positioned better than ever to address this simple
education.

The recession of 2008 is perhaps an even more profound
voice for urban farming than the public health correlation.
Across the country, cities were quickly decimated by the burst
of the housing bubble. Entire communities were vacated and
unemployment rates skyrocketed. Major industries collapsed

and municipalities that depended on them were left with limited alternatives. Urban farming is being seen as one of a few bright spots in an otherwise still somewhat bleak economic outlook. With relatively little capital investment, unemployed citizens can turn vacant land into something productive in a relatively short time.

Food Safety

The last trend that has given urban farming a big push is related to food safety. Over the last century, staggering numbers of family farms have been consolidated by corporations. Today, only a handful of corporations process the majority of our food, and an only slightly larger handful of farms produce that food. Because food prices have remained steady and few health problems have occurred, the public has paid little attention to this conglomeration. This all began to change in 2006, as one food-borne epidemic after another rocketed through the country. Everyone was quick to play a blame game and shirk responsibility. Large corporate farms blamed small organic farms for letting manure into the food systems. Small organic farms blamed factory farms for not providing adequate sanitation for their farm workers. No one seemed to notice that the entire food system is at fault. Urban farms have risen to the top of the food security debate as one of the only ways to secure safe food. If your food comes from down the street, you can inspect it yourself, and if there's a problem, it's easy to detect. On the other hand, large-scale food production, without massive increases in regulatory spending, prohibits any measurable means to ensure food is safe and to track a problem if one occurs. A diversified web of small local growers in close contact with their customers is a simple solution.

Who Is Farming?

One blazing hot day during the first summer I worked transforming a vacant lot into Jones Valley Urban Farm, I noticed a bunch of kids from the surrounding neighborhood climbing a tree tucked between a nearby shed and a fence. As a responsible organizational director, I went over to tell them that climbing in the tree was a liability and that they needed to go back across the street to the playground. As I got closer to the tree, I was shocked to see that their faces were covered with the blue juice of the mulberry. For years, these kids had been coming to this lot at this time each summer to feast on the mulberries. I was struck at how our efforts to cultivate a vacant lot into a food-production site had neglected to even notice this prolific weed tree growing quietly in the corner. The kids knew better.

The explosion of local farmer's markets is creating easier avenues for these farmers to sell their products directly to the consumer, and thereby actually make a living.

The Power to Plant

Marilyn Nefer Ra Barber, who currently runs Detroit's D-Town Farm, is one of the many urban farmers we met across the country in the summer of 2010. Like many southerners over the last century, she moved north to Detroit in part to escape farm life. "Most of the people in Detroit left farms in the South," she says, "and they didn't want anything to do with the farm. Now we're almost at the point where we're forced into it again, but this time it's to gain the power to plant that seed and control your food. When you see it that way, you have to give the farm a second chance." Although Marilyn's experience with farming in the city is common from New York to Seattle, it is not the only story. When looking at who is farming in cities in America, it might be easier to ask who is *not* farming. . . .

You can literally find somebody from every demographic farming in the city. Marginalized African American communities are turning blighted vacant lots into community farms that bring power back into their local economies. Immigrant communities are blending their traditional agricultural techniques into sustenance and market gardening. Affluent communities are planting in backyards and church lawns, often donating the produce to feed residents of local shelters.

Growing Profits

A growing trend among urban farmers goes back to an early incentive behind agriculture: to make a profit. Programs such as SPIN (small plot intensive farming) offer guidelines on how to turn small vacant lots into a viable income. The explosion of local farmer's markets is creating easier avenues for these farmers to sell their products directly to the consumer, and thereby actually make a living. In New Orleans, Marilyn Yank is experimenting with turning vacant corner lots into a neighborhood-supported farm. She supplies eight families with weekly produce from a tiny corner lot in downtown. She sees it as a simple experiment: "Can you make a living turning something wasted in the community into something healthy and productive? There's a formula that probably works. I'm trying to find out what it is."

Cracks in the Concrete

One of the more profound distinctions of urban farmers is that they are rarely trained in agriculture or even come from an agricultural background. While nearly all conventional rural growers are "inheriting" an agricultural tradition, most urban farmers are driven by philosophical motives to better their community or make a living. Even though many nonprofits are developing training programs and academic institutions are beginning to offer courses in urban agriculture, we still have a long way to go before a system is in place to match the opportunities in urban farming with the supply of knowledgeable practitioners.

2

Community Gardens Grow Strong Communities

Peter Ladner

Peter Ladner has served two terms as a city councillor in Vancouver, British Columbia, and has a longstanding interest in the relationship between food policy and city planning.

Gardening brings people together in a way that few things do. Community gardens allow people from different backgrounds and who may not even speak the same language to share a common purpose and goal, and to build relationships amongst themselves. When this happens, it has an impact far beyond the garden itself. Besides strengthening understanding and communication between diverse elements of a community, gardens transform blighted public spaces and improve property values. They empower disenfranchised populations such as new immigrants and the poor, and there is even evidence that they help ease social problems, such as crime. While it can be difficult to secure land for a community garden, many cities are now supporting community garden endeavors because they acknowledge the many health, education, and community benefits that gardens create.

I once happened upon a community garden in Victoria, B.C. [British Columbia], a provincial capital renowned for its gardens. Ever curious about community gardens, I strolled in

Peter Ladner, "Growing Community with Community Gardens," *The Urban Food Revolution—Changing the Way We Feed Cities*. Gabriola Island, British Columbia: New Society, 2011, pp. 181–187, 190–193, 195. Copyright © 2011 by New Society Publishers. All rights reserved. Reproduced by permission.

and looked around. I had never seen such a neat, well-ordered community garden. Although these gardens typically express the various states of unruliness of their plot-holders, this one had little picket fences; there were no weeds in the pathways, and everything was neat and tidy. This even extended to the notice board, which in some gardens is nothing more than a scrawled notice on a piece of plywood saying "Please respect our gardeners. Don't pick what isn't yours." This garden had posted rules, notices and regulations, all evenly spaced and up-to-date. Meticulously typed minutes from the most recent meeting of the society's officers were posted. Citations for members who hadn't been properly attending their plots were listed in the minutes, along with a description of escalating penalties given in grinding detail.

As is usual in these gardens, there was someone around who loves to talk, even at 7:30 in the morning. A man tending his plot was glad to answer my questions. "This is an exceptionally well-organized garden," I commented. "That's because most of the gardens are used by former public servants with backgrounds in drafting legislation and crafting public policy," he answered with a wry smile. "We have an abundance of policy enthusiasm."

Urban community garden food production has ebbed and waned in the United States in tune with food shortages caused by depression or wars.

A Garden Reflects Its Community

Every community garden has its own enthusiasms that reflect its community. The Eagle Heights Community Garden at the University of Wisconsin has gardeners who speak more than 60 languages among them. Gardeners can fill out application forms in four languages: English, Spanish, Chinese or Korean.

When I dropped by the community garden at the sprawling farm at the Intervale, in Burlington, Vermont, I spotted a policy enthusiasm of another sort. An older Chevy S-10 pickup was parked by the entrance, its tailgate emblazoned with bumper stickers espousing every progressive cause imaginable. As I wondered what the owner would look like, I caught the eye of an older man in shorts and a T-shirt, digging soil into a newly framed raised plot. In the tradition of everybody being friends inside a community garden, I started asking him questions, and he eagerly told me about his involvement, which had lasted two decades. I commented on the truck nearby. "That's mine," he said proudly. Then he introduced himself: "I'm Robert Kiss. I'm the mayor of Burlington."

Gardens Born of Necessity

Community gardens aren't new. They emerge in periods when people are threatened by food insecurity. Urban community garden food production has ebbed and waned in the United States in tune with food shortages caused by depression or wars. Detroit Mayor Hazen Pingree initiated "potato patches" to help Detroit citizens through the 1893 depression. During World War I the US federal government organized War Gardens. Work relief gardens and cooperative farms were created during the Great Depression of the 1930s. World War II brought the Victory Garden campaign to the United States, Canada, Britain and other countries. At their peak, Victory Gardens in the United States may have accounted for as much as 40% of the vegetable production in the country....

Later in the 20th century, community gardens as we know them today began to spring up as part of grassroots urban movements, resulting in the establishment of the American Community Gardening Association in 1978, with members across the United States and Canada. Today's community gardens are a mix of private allotment plots and larger, shared gardens usually organized by a community group. The shared social experience of gardening is a big focus, but most gardeners are also interested in growing their own food. Typically, food is not grown commercially in community gardens, although some gardeners do sell their produce.

Today's Models

The four goals of the University of Wisconsin's Eagle Heights Community Gardens illustrate the range of interest of today's community gardeners: nutrition, recreation, education and community building.

Montreal is just one city with a proud explosion of community gardens. It has more than 100 gardens, each with an average of 30 parking space-sized plots. Sustainlane, the online "People-Powered Sustainability Guide," ranked Minneapolis as the top US city for farmers markets and community gardens per capita (sustainlane.com).

Troy Gardens in Madison, Wisconsin, claims to have the second-biggest community garden complex on the continent (after nearby University of Wisconsin's Eagle Heights, which has more than 500 plots and 1,000 gardeners. But it's been going since 1962). Troy Gardens' 327 good-sized plots (20 feet by 20 feet) are broken up into more than 30 different "gardens," which are all part of a wonderfully integrated 31-acre development that includes 30 units of co-housing, a five-acre farm providing produce for CSA [community supported agriculture] members, and a five-acre restored natural area that's burned off every year. The co-housing residents are also worker-caretakers who keep their eyes and ears on the gardens. Many have their own garden plots and help as volunteers for work parties and special events. The rest of the work is done by five full-time-equivalent employees, 30-plus volunteer interns, and hundreds of other volunteers.

The Common Language of Gardening

Acting Executive Director Christie Ralston showed me around the snow-covered site on a bright January day. She had her white wool hat pulled down low, and she smiled a lot as she talked proudly about what happened there when everything was growing. "This garden is a great equalizer," she noted. "When Mung women come here, they're speaking the common language of gardening, like everyone else."

Gardeners love to talk about their plants, and community gardens can get conversations started.

Christie's gardeners speak English, Spanish, Mung and Lao. Some of her favorite visitors are the forensic mental patients who come here on day passes with a nurse. She also hosts teenage youths on day passes from a nearby jail. "They hate being out in nature, but when I give them hard, heavy work to do and they see results, they like it." The visitation programs connect visitors with nature through the gardens. For the younger kids, it sometimes means just digging in the dirt, never mind what kind of hole they're making. "I particularly remember one of the teenage boys tell me after we had done some sampling and pointing out different plants: 'I smelled things I had never smelled before.'"

Planting "Community" into Community Gardens

One of my first awakenings to the myriad benefits of community gardens was when the community police officer in a troubled neighborhood in Vancouver helped get one started. She wanted a project for the homeless people hanging around the neighborhood. They embraced it eagerly—a chance to care for something, do something positive, to witness the fruits (actually, vegetables) of their labor. She said the only problem was that so many people wanted to water the plants all the time.

Community gardens contribute to safety by getting people into the street for hours at a time. "Eyes and ears on the street" make streets safe.

Gardeners love to talk about their plants, and community gardens can get conversations started. A friend of mine who started growing vegetables on the city-owned boulevard outside her house (encouraged in Vancouver and some other cities) said hardly anyone walked by without stopping to chat.

Transforming Blighted Space

Another community garden in Vancouver is on an abandoned lot a block away from the highest-crime transit station in the city. It used to be littered with needles and condoms. Today, it's a proud little garden. Once when I went by, I talked to a gaunt, strung-out young woman. Her red nail polish was chipped, and she wore a black mock-leather coat as she squatted at the edge of a raised bed, carefully repotting vegetable seedlings in a zoned-out kind of way. She said she came to the garden and did these little tasks because it made her feel good.

You don't need a lot of skill to do something useful at a community garden, and you don't have to commit a lot of time to produce results you can actually see.

Studies have shown that the presence of vegetable gardens in inner-city neighborhoods is positively correlated with decreases in crime, trash dumping, juvenile delinquency, fires, violent deaths, and mental illness.

Another community garden in Vancouver's poorest neighborhood—home to the city's highest concentration of low-income housing and drug addiction—is a little oasis of green between two older buildings that are continually struggling for retail tenants. It has to be kept fenced off most of the time, but at least it's there, growing a bit of food, bringing a flicker of green pride to a destitute street.

Community Gardens Raise Property Values

The transformation of a blighted abandoned property into a community garden has a measurable economic impact. A study in New York found that opening a community garden increases property values ("a statistically significant positive impact") within 1,000 feet of the garden. And the impact increases over time. The biggest changes are in the most disadvantaged neighborhoods, and with the highest quality gardens.

A similar study in Milwaukee found that residents are willing to pay more to live near a community garden, driving up the market value of properties within a three-block radius of a community garden. That study went so far as to calculate the increased taxes to the city from the higher property values. They calculated that the average community garden contributes $8,880 in annual tax revenue to a city.

Other studies have shown that the presence of vegetable gardens in inner-city neighborhoods is positively correlated with decreases in crime, trash dumping, juvenile delinquency, fires, violent deaths, and mental illness. A simpler and more measurable economic impact of community gardens is the money saved in mowing and maintenance costs when a volunteer-run garden takes over space in a publicly financed park.

Health authorities concerned about soaring costs of obesity and diabetes love community gardens. They directly address the two main solutions to those epidemics: exercise and better diet. Research shows that urban gardeners and their families consume more fruits and vegetables, have reduced grocery bills, and supply culturally valued fruits and vegetables in ethnic communities. (To keep the money-savings in perspective, though, keep in mind this comment from a woman tending her plot in a beautiful seaside garden in White Rock, B.C.: "I'm certainly not doing this to save money—I spent as much on my organic bean seeds as it costs me to buy a big bag of fresh organic beans from Costco.")

Community Gardens as Political Power

Community gardens can also give new immigrants a chance to position themselves as local experts. In Montreal, a McGill University project called Making the Edible Landscape found that immigrants from India and Bangladesh came to community gardens with agricultural knowledge that enabled them to drastically increase a plot's yield (such as building trellises to triple available growing space).

Some disenfranchised groups see community gardens as a path to political power. "In Detroit, a lot of gardeners do it for political reasons—it's a slap in the face for agri-business, and a way to control their own food security," says Monica White, a sociology professor at Wayne State University. "Growing food is a way for African Americans to engage in a struggle for freedom. Resistance usually acts against institutions. With gardening, we take the initiative into our own hands."

The most secure gardens are ones that have made their way onto public lands already protected from development.

Malik Yakini chairs the Detroit Black Community Food Security Network, an organization that operates D-Town, two acres of gardens in the largest park in the city, on land leased from the city for 10 years. Yakini, speaking at the Farm to Cafeteria conference in May 2010 said, "In most cities, community garden work is being done in black and Latino communities mostly by young white people with a missionary mentality. . . . We speak openly about white supremacy. We're unabashed advocates for self-sufficiency in the Afro-American community."

Self-Sufficiency

Self-sufficiency means food, and a study in Philadelphia showed community gardens grow a lot of it, even though most gardens are broken up into separately managed small plots, not geared for high production. All the same, a University of Pennsylvania research team found 220 food-producing community gardens in the city in 2008; an estimated 2.2 million pounds of food was produced, worth around $4.4 million. Most of it wasn't grown for sale: "The majority of gardeners in low-wealth communities distribute a significant proportion of their harvest to extended family, neighbors, fellow church members, and strangers who are hungry," writes Professor Domenic Vitiello.

The Earlscourt Park Community Garden in Toronto is a consolidated community garden: a single 8,000-square foot garden that is geared to food production. Community members grow, tend and harvest more than 2,000 pounds of organic produce for use in The Stop's food distribution programs.

Finding Space for Community Gardens

Even with all the well-known advantages of community gardens, finding space for them in crowded cities with competing claims on land is often a big challenge. Particularly vexing is security of tenure: who wants to build up a garden and then see it shut down?

The most secure gardens are ones that have made their way onto public lands already protected from development— parks, schools and rights of way for power lines or sewer access. Park gardens often have to struggle against the argument that public land is being appropriated for private use by a self-selected group of gardeners. I understand this concern, but look at the result: volunteers will keep a portion of the park maintained, and they provide conversation, creative landscaping and interactive viewing for visitors who want to come into the gardens and visit and poke around. So who really cares?

Actually, one group who cares is park and school workers. Some of their unions see community gardeners as people who are taking over their jobs by providing volunteer labor. The same arguments can be heard when schools want to put in gardens. I know of one school where unionized staff insisted on being the primary garden builders, which cost the school's parents far more money than if they had been allowed to build the garden themselves.

The benefits of these gardens are so manifold and obvious that these turf issues will become irrelevant in the long run, especially if a garden has a wide enough coalition of supporters.

The city of Oakland moved in the direction of an Urban Land Trust when City Slicker Farms accessed $4 million in 2010 for acquiring land to grow food on. The funds were part of a $5.4 billion California state bond for projects involving water quality and access, park improvements, and natural resource and park preservation. Barbara Finnin, executive director of City Slicker Farms, described the grant as a game-changer: "It's painful to put big infrastructure in and not have the land for very long."

Temporary Gardens Find New Homes

Community gardens deliver their biggest added value when they're sited in places that are not already green and protected—places like parking lots and abandoned industrial sites. This is where tenure gets tricky: demand for these lands evolves, and sometimes it's hard to justify keeping a farm going on valuable property. But what if the gardeners don't want to leave?

In Vancouver, developers discovered that turning their vacant lots into community gardens while they waited for their next project to be ready could save them hundreds of thousands of dollars in city taxes. Putting a garden on a commercially zoned site allows it to be reclassified as public park or garden, resulting in an 80% tax saving—even if it is known that the garden is temporary. In one downtown property where a hotel parking lot was converted to an urban farm, the property owner is saving $132,000 a year in taxes. (Under Vancouver's tax policies, this money isn't lost to the city; it's parceled out among the remaining commercial property taxpayers.)

As a result of this discovery, developer-financed community gardens have popped up in prominent downtown locations to the delight of many. . . .

The Two-Block Diet Garden

Two neighbors in Vancouver have put together a new kind of community garden. It's made up of the backyards of residents in two city blocks. It started with a flyer asking neighbors if they had land available for growing food. Thirteen people showed up for a meeting. They started teaming up to plant and weed each other's backyards. That led to potluck dinners, a bee hive, some chicken coops, a shared greenhouse, a neighborhood compost operation, canning parties, and harvests two and three times bigger than they were before.

"We share tools, organize large purchases of seeds, compost and rentals together to lower fees," says Kate Sutherland, one of the organizers. "Each week we go to one person's garden to tackle a large project that would take a single person at least a day or two to do themselves. The results have been quite dramatic, visually and emotionally. We've all been blown away by how simple, effective and fulfilling this has been. We can't imagine going back to the way things were before our mini garden revolution."

Like so many community gardeners, she says the real payoff has been in the sense of community that's been created. "I lived on this block for 12 years and had never been inside most of my neighbors' homes; now I have been in all of the members' homes."

They've even produced a manual, *The Two-Block Diet: An Unmanual.* It includes the caution that "each neighborhood is different, and only you will know if things are going to work in your area." . . .

Community gardens satisfy so many needs in our communities that gardeners, police, seniors' centers, corporations and cities are lining up to be involved with them. They usually have other goals than simply providing food, but they invariably provide food. That's why they've been around since the 1800s, and why so many more people are getting interested in them in today's times of economic distress. So much the better that they also provide healthy activities, education and community building. Finding space for them is getting easier as their benefits become better known.

3

Urban Farming Improves Access to Healthy Food

Elizabeth Limbach

Elizabeth Limbach is the news editor at Good Times, *an alternative weekly newspaper in Santa Cruz, California.*

Soaring rates of obesity and type 2 diabetes are a growing public health crisis in the United States. But the effects of these conditions go far beyond health; they impact the economy, too, with skyrocketing healthcare costs and loss of productivity at work and school. Because these conditions are strongly diet related, many people believe that increasing access to healthy foods— especially for the poor—can help turn the problem around. Food banks that serve the needy are shifting away from providing processed and packaged foods and are increasing the amount of fresh fruits and vegetables that they distribute. Community garden programs and gardens in schools are an effective way to increase a community's access to fresh produce. Teaching children and families how to grow and prepare fresh foods promotes healthier eating and a healthier community.

Longtime doctors, like Donaldo Hernandez, MD, have watched from the front row as our nation has ballooned at the waistline over the years.

"You can see the shift—it's not subtle," says Hernandez, a hospital physician for the Palo Alto Medical Foundation and past president of the Santa Cruz County Medical Society. "I see the effect of it every day in the hospital, when people get admitted with respiratory abnormalities, sleep apnea, diabetes, coronary disease, pulmonary disease, and other things related to obesity."

The fact that a quarter of kids between 5 and 19 years old are obese in Santa Cruz County, according to the Centers for Disease Control, doesn't bode well for those individuals, but it also spells bad news for the community as a whole.

As they grow up grappling with diet-related health problems, school performance can suffer and, ultimately, so can work opportunities and performance.

"What it means is you don't do well in school, it's more difficult for you to get a job, to keep a job, and, in addition, you have high medical costs," explains Willy Elliot-McCrea, CEO of Second Harvest Food Bank (SHFB). "The costs of managing diabetes, asthma and heart conditions that come from obesity are very expensive. It's one of the big things that is driving poverty and family bankruptcy. It creates a cycle of, and sets up the next generation of, hunger and poverty."

The Link to Diabetes

One in three Americans born in 2000 will be diagnosed with type 2 diabetes, which can lead to renal failure, blindness, and other complications, by the age of 25 according to the American Diabetes Association. This figure goes up to 50 percent for Latinos and African Americans.

In addition to the healthcare costs that local economies must absorb, obesity-related conditions have indirect costs, such as decreasing worker productivity.

Last year, the Association reported a 41 percent increase in the total costs incurred by diabetes in the country from $174 billion in 2007 to $245 billion in 2012.

The price for our communities is high—and increasingly ominous, says California Sen. Bill Monning.

"In addition to the healthcare costs that local economies must absorb, obesity-related conditions have indirect costs, such as decreasing worker productivity," he says.

Health-related issues in the workforce lead to $100 to $150 billion lost annually in the United States, says Workforce Investment Board of Santa Cruz County Director David Mirrione.

"Productivity gains can result in higher profitability for businesses and can create both the need and means to increase the size of their workforce," he says, noting that he believes implementation of the Affordable Care Act, by increasing healthcare coverage, will aid in this.

Healthy food is the ticket to preventing these problems from worsening, says Hernandez, who is part of the SHFB-organized Business Leadership Forum, which gathers leaders from the business community to focus on the issue. There are colossal forces at work that make this sensible solution far from simple. (Think: federal subsidies for "all the wrong foods," in Hernandez's words; massive junk- and fast-food advertising campaigns targeted at children; ubiquitous food deserts barring those who need healthy food from accessing it; and Congress' inability to pass a Farm Bill, threatening the federal food assistance program.)

But, in the meantime, grassroots endeavors chip away at the issue. Here, we take a look at [two] of many local efforts making a dent. [Both] aim to reduce the societal implications of poor health—one, SHFB's Passion for Produce program, by educating low-income residents about nutrition and healthy cooking, and the other, Mesa Verde Gardens, by increasing access to produce through the proliferation of affordable community garden plots. . . .

The Education Element

When Second Harvest Food Bank started out in Santa Cruz County in the early '70s, hunger meant a lack of calories—and a food bank's job was to provide those calories. It's not so simple anymore.

Paradoxically, today, hunger can mean obesity. Against a backdrop of fast food and junk food that's often cheaper than healthier choices, hunger means an overabundance of the wrong calories, or "non-nutritive" calories. It means a whole generation of poor children who are overfed but malnourished; who will have to deal with health complications from diet-related conditions such as obesity and diabetes for years to come.

As the nature of hunger in this country has changed, so has SHFB's mission. What once was as straightforward as providing emergency food assistance is evolving into "nutrition banking." More than 60 percent of the food bank's distribution is now fresh produce.

Passion for Produce recruits ambassadors and participants through outreach to low-income communities in the county, including farmworkers, who are often food insecure despite working in agriculture.

But is providing healthy fruits and vegetables to low-income clients enough to improve their diets, or is some education necessary? According to 60 percent of Second Harvest clients surveyed in 2006, nutrition classes, recipes and cooking demonstrations would be a welcomed service.

Based on that input, the organization launched its Passion for Produce program in 2009. In it, 260 trained peer leaders, called "nutrition ambassadors," lead monthly classes at 28 sites countywide.

"First and foremost, we wanted it to be a program that would empower the community to take control of their and their family's health for themselves," says Brooke Johnson, chief operations and programs officer for SHFB. "We provide training so nutrition ambassadors can be out front in the community really leading the charge for people to make healthier choices."

Passion for Produce

Passion for Produce recruits ambassadors and participants through outreach to low-income communities in the county, including farmworkers, who are often food insecure despite working in agriculture. More than half of program participants are farmworker households.

The nutritional and cooking information provided aims to show that "even people who are low income and on a budget can make different choices within the resources they have," says Johnson.

When SHFB volunteer and Capitola resident Leona Lail was approached about becoming a nutrition ambassador, she said no. "I said that it—that role—wasn't me," she says, "and that I'd rather just volunteer."

But, after being persuaded and embarking on the six-week training course required of ambassadors, Lail realized that her own health and that of her family was improving, and that she had the opportunity to pass that on to others in the community.

Lail has always loved to cook, and often made her own twists on dishes she saw made on the Food Network. She says that her experience with Passion for Produce has given her the tools to make healthier versions of meals she was already cooking. Instead of ambrosia salad, which pairs fruit with whipped cream and marshmallows, she opts for fresh fruit salads, for example.

"I can tell by looking at what's on my grocery bill that I'm eating healthier," she says. "Before, I used to get quick things for me and my kids. Now, when shopping, I think to do salad and a smaller piece of protein, or a stir-fry or vegetable soup. And I read more labels than I ever did."

Although each family walks away from a Passion for Produce class with 25 pounds of fresh produce, the program is equally about teaching attendees how to utilize those healthy foods. Together with an SHFB representative, nutrition ambassadors like Lail build the classes around what is in that week's donation bag. At first, Lail noticed that many attendees were coming just for the food assistance. But, over time, she says most are won over by the educational aspect.

The [Passion for Produce] program is currently reaching between 1,110 and 1,500 people a month—that's a lot of opportunity for healthier individuals, but also a healthier community overall.

Teaching New Habits

"When you show them other options, let them taste it, and give them the recipe . . . they take that and actually use it," she says. "They go home and do make that kind of food, using less oils, less sugar, less salts and more natural fruits and vegetables."

Both Johnson and Lail report that many participants have lost weight since starting Passion for Produce, and Lail is optimistic that they will continue to eat healthily once they stop attending and are no longer receiving the free bag of produce.

"The price of everything has gone up so high," she says, "and we've discussed how to economize in a healthy way. For example, it's hard to buy enough meat for everyone if you have a family of five, so how can you use more vegetables and other types of proteins like healthy grains or beans?"

The program is currently reaching between 1,110 and 1,500 people a month—that's a lot of opportunity for healthier individuals, but also a healthier community overall, says Johnson.

"We are trying to work with our volunteers and partner sites to help create a healthier community so that kids can concentrate and succeed in school, so parents can be productive at work," she says, "and so that it's one less thing for people to have to worry about when they are looking for a job and doing other things to move their family forward."

As a nutrition bank, this is also SHFB's broader goal.

"Altogether, through our network of 200 member agencies, we reach 55,000 people a month," Johnson says. "That's a lot of folks in our community who are struggling with being able to afford food at some point during the month. Think of that human potential: that's almost a quarter of the people in our county. It makes us stronger as a community countywide when everyone can do their best in work or school or in looking for employment."

Addressing Access

When, after 20 years of doing social work in Santa Cruz County, Ana Rasmussen felt called to a career in the sustainable food movement, she couldn't shake her social worker nature.

This led her to what she feels is an intersection of these two fields—food justice. Her mission became reducing diet-related health problems, like obesity and diabetes, in low-income communities through increased access to produce.

Rasmussen founded the nonprofit Mesa Verde Gardens, which kicked off its garden program in March 2010 with a raised-bed garden at the Martinelli Head Start preschool in Watsonville. Soon there were 10 preschool gardens, all at schools that serve low-income populations.

However, while the gardens worked well for educating kids about healthy foods, they weren't doing much to improve access—two raised beds, for example, means each of 60 preschoolers [is] getting "two peas and a tomato," Rasmussen says, half-jokingly.

"If the point is really to impact the obesity and diabetes epidemic and make an impact on food insecurity, then that's not much food," she says.

The next step for Mesa Verde Gardens happened organically.

Expanding the Program

"One day I was just driving to that first preschool site, putting away a wheelbarrow," explains Rasmussen. "I was noticing that they had a lot of land there. I needed some help and I saw someone and asked her if she would help me with the wheelbarrow. We started talking, she said she was the priest. I said 'I was looking at that land, I was wondering if we could start a community gar—,' I didn't even finish my sentence. She shook my hand and said 'Let's do it.' It was that easy. It fell into existence."

Community orchards are becoming more popular around the country.

That garden quickly filled to capacity with 30 families, who began growing in 2011. Now there are three community gardens—all pesticide-free—that serve 110 families. As part of Rasmussen's health-related mission, it is a requirement that all participants have a child they share the produce with. A fourth garden is on its way at the Santa Cruz County Fairgrounds through a partnership with the Agricultural History Project, and the latest addition is an orchard behind Lutheran Community Church in Watsonville.

Rasmussen looks out over the sloping orchard lined with small, young trees that were planted in February [2013]. In time, they will grow to be welcomed sources of apples, pears, stone fruit and citrus for Mesa Verde participants.

"Community orchards are becoming more popular around the country," Rasmussen says. "[Participants are] growing vegetables already, so now there will be organic fruit, too." She expects to have another two orchards planted by next year.

Less than a mile away, at All Saints Episcopal Church on Rogers Avenue in Watsonville, 6-year-old Michael Ortega romps through the aisles of his family's fertile plot at Mesa Verde Gardens' largest, and first, community garden site.

He plucks a ripe tomato from the vine and munches on it like an apple. When asked if he helps his mother, Angelica Ortega, with the gardening, he nods shyly. "I help with something else, too," he adds. "I help with the eating." At that, he skips over to the row of green beans and snaps off a pod.

Small Plots with Big Results

The plot is brimming with tomatillos, spinach, zucchini, chilies, cucumbers, beets and more. The rest of the garden's 54 plots are similarly abundant on this July day, making it easy to see how families averaged 47 pounds of produce a month last year, according to Rasmussen. At $5 per month to rent a plot (plus a two-hour monthly work commitment), this makes for a great deal on organic produce, says Angelica, who has rented her plot since the garden started three years ago.

She says her family saved hundreds in grocery expenses last year. And, by learning to can vegetables through Mesa Verde Gardens last summer, they were able to stretch their bountiful summer yield through what would have otherwise been a tough winter.

"It's hard to find organic produce in Watsonville, and it's expensive," Angelica says. "So I keep renting this space. It's very affordable, it's all organic, and it's helping our family a lot—they are learning to eat more vegetables."

Angelica was precisely the type of person Rasmussen had in mind when founding Mesa Verde Gardens—she was interested in growing her own food, but lacked the space to do so.

"Where I grew up in Salamanca, Mexico, I used to garden, but not here," she says. "We live in an apartment. We don't have any space [for gardening], not even for a plant."

A tomato's throw from her plot are the gardens of her father, who is diabetic, and her sister, who works as a fieldworker. Angelica is helping tend their gardens while her father copes with some health problems and her sister is busy working six-day workweeks.

It's beyond ironic. How could it be in an agricultural community that people don't have access to produce?

Fieldworkers Have Garden Know-How

Around 70 percent of Mesa Verde Gardens' families consist of at least one fieldworker, says Rasmussen. The paradoxical fact that the very same people who grow the area's copious agricultural crops have poor access to fresh produce inspired Rasmussen when founding the program.

"It's beyond ironic. How could it be in an agricultural community that people don't have access to produce? But rural communities are hit just as hard as inner city communities on that access," she says. "I wanted to figure out how I could impact that in some small way."

Similar projects in urban communities, like a program Rasmussen previously worked with in Oakland, also address the lack of healthy foods in these so-called food deserts. But one big difference Rasmussen has encountered in operating community gardens in an agricultural area is that the learning curve for participants is drastically reduced—or even nonexistent.

"When I worked in Oakland, there was a lot of really basic teaching," she says. "Here, you provide the land and get out of the way because people really know what they're doing. I've learned so much from people who know so much about growing food."

As for whether the gardens are improving the community's health, as she hopes, Rasmussen says that's hard to confirm.

"I've heard that it's hard to prove that," she says, "because, if someone has a plot, then maybe they get a yield and maybe they don't, maybe they take it home or they don't, maybe it rots at home, maybe they eat it . . . but I don't think people who have really full lives are going to spend that time to grow food and then let it go to waste."

Mesa Verde Gardens had an 82 percent retention rate last year, meaning most gardeners renewed their membership for another year. And in surveys, a majority of participants report eating more produce than they did previously, which suggests that their diets have become healthier.

"Health is what it's all pinned on," says Rasmussen. "If you aren't healthy, you have a lot fewer options. Everyone should have access to a good, healthy diet and it shouldn't have anything to do with your income. This program creates an opportunity for people to help themselves."

Mesa Verde Gardens may be a "shoestring" operation that relies on grants and donations, but Rasmussen says her work won't be over until everyone who wants to grow their own food can do so.

4

Urban Farms Clash with Cities over Regulations

Anna Toon

Food journalist Anna Toon writes the On the Range *food blog for* The Austin Chronicle *website and is a contributor to the newspaper's food and books sections.*

HausBar Farms, an urban farm in Austin, Texas, is seen by many people as a model for "responsible and sustainable agriculture." But when a neighbor complained about a smelly compost pile, it launched a whole series of investigations by various city departments. Now, the farm is shut down and the owners find themselves stuck in a bureaucratic maze with no clear end in sight. The situation at HausBar Farms illustrates the complex, confusing, or contradictory regulations that often underlie the relationship between cities and urban farmers, especially those who keep animals. It also underscores a criticism of many: that urban farms represent a form of gentrification in established residential areas. Clear municipal regulations are needed to protect the interests of those on both sides of the issue.

The Austin City Council will soon be asked to revisit what it means to be an urban farm. For everything from increased access to locally produced foods to reduced crime rates, many look to urban farms to resolve issues of food insecurity in low-income neighborhoods. Austin's burgeoning urban agriculture movement provides ample opportunities to positively impact the community at large. According to TXP economist Jon Hockenyos, in a report commissioned by City Council to address urban agriculture and local food systems, "If local farmers and food artisans are able to produce and sell more to Austin consumers, restaurants, and institutional buyers, each will benefit to the gain of the overall community." Despite this, activists and residents alike have concerns about how the propagation of urban farms contributes to gentrification and land-use planning issues.

HausBar Farms, conceived by Dorsey Barger and Susan Hausmann in 2009, is widely considered a model for responsible and sustainable agriculture. Barger originally made her mark on the Eastside as the original co-owner and operator of Eastside Cafe. In 2011, Barger sold her share in the eatery to co-owner Elaine Martin in order to focus her attention on farming. She and Hausmann have now revitalized almost two acres of land on the Eastside into a working urban farm. Previously a fallow lot, the farm now boasts chickens, donkeys, rabbits, geese, and a bounty of vegetables. However, in recent months, Barger has been accused of exploiting the neighborhood through environmental injustice.

An Unexpected Opponent

What started as an unpleasant odor has since escalated into an entanglement involving multiple city departments and state agencies. Further complicating the issue is the involvement of environmental justice group People Organized in Defense of Earth and Her Resources (PODER). While an urban farm may seem an unlikely target for environmental activists, PODER accused HausBar Farms of operating commercially in a residential zone and gentrifying the area surrounding the farm. According to PODER's Daniel Llanes, the activist group had to tackle the issue because other environmental groups wouldn't touch it: "HausBar Farms and the whole urban farm movement is generally a white movement, and so here's where it clashes. You don't see SOS [Save Our Springs] over here, or Sierra Club."

Historically, PODER has worked to move industries and environmental hazards out of residential areas and, specifically, out of East Austin's communities of color. PODER takes credit for the relocation of the East Austin tank farm, a 52-acre storage-tank area owned by six major oil companies, including Exxon, Citgo, and Texaco. The tank farm, located at the corner of Airport Boulevard and Springdale Road, had been contaminating the ground water and had been linked to illness in the surrounding area. In recent months, the activist group has turned its attention to HausBar Farms, lodging a barrage of complaints against the farm.

After an interdepartmental inspection ... city officials shut down HausBar Farms, citing inadequate permits; inconsistencies in the urban farm ordinance surely must have impacted the decision, as well.

In late November [2012], Louis Polanco, a 50-year resident of the Govalle/Johnston Terrace neighborhood, called Austin 311 to complain about a foul smell. The stench was coming from a black soldier fly composter that is adjacent to the processing facilities at HausBar Farms, across the street from Polanco's home. This self-contained composting system utilizes black soldier fly larvae to break down farm scraps. In doing so, unutilized farm products are rapidly transformed into a low-cost and highly sustainable source of protein for chickens.

Complaint Prompts Inspections

HausBar Farms is not the only Eastside farm to utilize black soldier fly compost, as it is extremely efficient. However, on this particular day, the compost was out of balance and generating the foul odor. Though HausBar had been slaughtering chickens and composting the waste for two years with no incident at that point, Polanco's complaint spurred a series of inspections by multiple city departments, including the City of Austin Planning and Development Review Department, Austin/Travis County Health Department, City of Austin Code Compliance, and the City of Austin Watershed Protection Department.

During this time, Polanco took his complaints to *YNN News* and the *Austin American-Statesman*, then reached out to Susana Almanza and Daniel Llanes of PODER. On Feb. 28 [2013], Almanza and Llanes spoke in front of City Council during the citizen communication portion of the meeting. Almanza began by portraying zoning and land-use planning as one of the most powerful tools employed in the cause of racism. While not opposed to urban farms in general, Almanza went on to describe the activities of HausBar Farms as exceeding the intent of urban farm land use in a residential area. Llanes specifically opposed the slaughtering of chickens to be sold commercially, characterizing HausBar as a "mass production" operation, slaughtering up to 50 chickens a day and risking harm to the neighborhood environment.

Barger strongly disputed these claims, contending that at the height of her operation, she processed about 20 chickens a week, far from the 250 per week suggested by Llanes. Despite the factual inconsistencies in PODER's presentation, the organization's testimony prompted further scrutiny by city officials. After an interdepartmental inspection on March 13, city officials shut down HausBar Farms, citing inadequate permits; inconsistencies in the urban farm ordinance surely must have impacted the decision, as well.

Zoning Conundrums

HausBar Farms is zoned SF-3, or single-family residential. Under SF-3, an urban farm is an approved use. In fact, urban farming is an approved use under all residential zoning districts, assuming certain requirements are met. While HausBar Farms is zoned correctly to operate as an urban farm, according to the city, they do not meet all of the requirements to operate as an urban farm.

Austin City Code 25-2-863 relating to urban farms permits farmers to raise fowl, including the processing/slaughtering of said fowl, and to sell the agricultural products from the site. At first glance, HausBar would appear to be operating within the appropriate guidelines. However, the trouble is with a seemingly insignificant provision: Section E of the code clearly states that one dwelling is permitted. Planning and Development has interpreted this section to mean an urban farm may have only one dwelling.

The sustainable Food Policy Board is working on language to lessen the restrictions on urban farms, especially concerning livestock, farm size, employees, and dwellings.

According to Barger, prior to their purchase of the property, plans were being made to turn the land into a 26-unit condominium. When Barger and Hausmann acquired the property, the existing structures were dilapidated, uninhabitable crack houses, so the couple moved a 780-square-foot cottage onto the property and renovated it. This plan was submitted to Residential Building Review and approved. After the older structures were repurposed into a hen house and barn, and the garage was converted into a commercial kitchen/poultry processing facility, Barger and Hausmann obtained all the necessary city permits for the construction of their dream home on the back of the property. Although no one at the city questioned this at the time the permits were issued, with the recent addition of this home, HausBar Farms no longer meets the one-dwelling requirement of the urban farm ordinance. In order to remedy this situation, city officials have proposed solutions ranging from subdividing the property to severing the utilities on the original front house, making it ultimately uninhabitable.

Permit Problems

Having two dwellings on the property isn't the only issue. HausBar is licensed through the Texas Department of Agriculture for the wholesale of graded eggs. Additionally, the farm has a rabbit and poultry exemption from the Texas Department of State Health Services [DSHS], allowing Barger to raise and slaughter rabbits and poultry and sell those products wholesale to chefs, restaurants, and caterers. However, Barger failed to obtain a building permit for her commercial kitchen/ processing facility. While DSHS inspected the farm's kitchen/ processing plant before issuing the rabbit and poultry exemption, the kitchen was not initially inspected by the Austin/ Travis County Health [and Human Services] Department. According to Barger, she thought the state inspection by DSHS was sufficient.

According to Vince Delisi, assistant division manager for the Austin/Travis County Health and Human Services Department, upon inspection of the kitchen, he found no health code violations and would like to work with other city departments to get Barger back in business. While she has since filed for the building permit to change the use of the garage into the processing facility, it is stuck in a backlog and may not be approved for months, during which time HausBar Farms will remain closed.

Regulations Need Revision

PODER, Barger, and all the city departments involved seem to agree on one matter: The urban farm ordinance needs to be rewritten and clarified. Currently, the Process and Code Coordination Working Group of the Sustainable Food Policy Board is working on language to lessen the restrictions on urban farms, especially concerning livestock, farm size, employees, and dwellings. Once the planning commission approves the amendments to the urban farm ordinance, it will go to City Council for approval. "We are currently working to propose a new, clear, streamlined urban farm code that protects farmers and their ability to make a living without getting bogged down in technicalities," explains Heather Frambach, research analyst and urban agriculture planner for the City of Austin's Sustainable Urban Agriculture & Community Gardens Program. "I am hopeful because this is precisely what our program was created to do: act as a strong liaison between communities, people who grow food, and the city."

Issues of zoning and ongoing gentrification will demand a continued discourse among farmers, the community, and city officials.

Throughout the entire ordeal, Barger received misinformation and confusing instructions from various city departments on how to proceed in order to become compliant with city regulations and the urban farm code. She was initially granted a change-of-use to operate as an urban farm, but it was rescinded as a result of the two dwellings. The permit process was confounded by a lack of communication between city departments, HausBar Farms, and PODER. In the end, frank and open dialogue must be encouraged in order to draft a new urban farm code that will sufficiently address critical issues and contribute to a secure future for urban agriculture.

For Barger, that moment can't come too soon. "We built our farm in good faith," she says. "We obtained the only licensing we were aware that we needed to have in order to process chickens and eggs from the state of Texas. We've proceeded in good faith in all of our efforts to start an urban farm with the city of Austin's blessing and now find ourselves unable to sell any of our product. . . . If we were able to get back in business while we go through the permitting process, we could make this work, but as much as individual departments in the city would like to help us, they've been unable to even tell us how to proceed to get into compliance."

No End to Conflict in Sight

Barger is working diligently with the city to meet the urban farm requirements, but even if she is allowed to reopen, PODER shows no signs of backing down. According to Almanza, the factual number of animals being processed is beside the point; PODER and neighbor Louis Polanco want that aspect of the operation stopped. Ultimately, issues of zoning and ongoing gentrification will demand a continued discourse among farmers, the community, and city officials. Says City Councilman Mike Martinez, "Urban farms are a way for us to address both sustainability and access to healthy food for our entire community. While we want to promote these types of activities, we also need to be mindful of what is suitable in the middle of a neighborhood. We'd like to keep a community dialogue going to determine what is and what isn't. I think of urban farms much like I think about home businesses. We have rules about running businesses out of your home, but we have to be mindful of the intensity of use and how they interact with the neighborhoods and uses around them."

As local food enthusiasts make plans for this weekend's East Austin Urban Farm Tour the future of HausBar Farms remains uncertain, though a meeting earlier this week between Llanes and Barger at HausBar Farms is an encouraging step. What is certain is that navigating the changing landscape of East Austin will be a balancing act between neighbors requiring both patience and perseverance.

5

The Butcher Next Door

James McWilliams

James McWilliams is an associate professor of history at Texas State University and the author of Just Food: Where Locavores Get It Wrong and How We Can Truly Eat Responsibly.

The killing of animals for food in urban areas is a problem for several reasons. The sights and sounds of suffering, dying animals is disturbing to most people, and the backyard slaughter of chickens, rabbits, goats, and other creatures is simply not an acceptable activity in residential areas. Additionally, keeping farm animals in urban backyards does not allow enough space for animals to behave naturally, and it can lead to the spread of diseases, such as salmonella. Although advocates for backyard husbandry say that animals are treated with care and dignity, even in their deaths, opponents maintain that performing or witnessing backyard animal slaughter desensitizes people to cruelty and that it is a barbaric and unnecessary practice that should be banned entirely.

When Armageddon strikes, it's a safe bet that Herrick Kimball will be serving chicken. Known as the Deliberate Agrarian, Kimball grew up "a sissified suburban kid" but decided at the age of 41 to toughen up, drop out of the corporate food system, and seek rural self-sufficiency. Slaughtering and butchering chickens—a multitude of chickens—is central to Kimball's evangelical quest to liberate himself from the corrupting influence of imported food. Culinarily, he's unplugged. Plugged in, however, is Kimball's computer, the pulpit from which he bangs out the gospel of poultry. His tutorial on how to properly butcher a chicken has earned well over a million hits.

Many of those hits have come from hip urban dwellers intent on controlling the food they eat. Urban farming has been happening as long as there have been urban centers, but only recently has it started to reincorporate animals into city space (something Americans stopped doing in the late 18th century due to sanitation concerns). The process began with egg-laying hens, which are now legal for residents to keep in most major cities in the United States. Now, however, urban überlocavores want to eat (and sell) not only eggs but also the chickens themselves, not to mention rabbits, ducks, goats, and even pigs. Municipal codes on keeping and slaughtering animals vary, but most of them are sufficiently vague for backyard butchers to quasi-legally hack the head off dinner within a few feet of the neighbors. A USDA survey found that 10 percent of residents in Denver, Los Angeles, Miami, and New York who keep chickens also kill them.

Urban centers already deal with plenty of daunting health and safety issues. Do we really want to add traditionally rural ones to the mix?

Decentralizing the act of animal slaughter in the name of taking back the food chain has an empowering ring to it. In reality, it's a fad rife with trouble. Advocates are quick to justify urban farming on the grounds that the industrial food system is broken. Compassionate carnivores aim to bypass the abattoir, eliminate the distance between farm and fork, and take full responsibility for the animals they eat. Do-it-yourself butchery is said to help eliminate food deserts, empower ethnic groups to maintain cultural traditions, and minimize animal suffering. It's billed as safer than industrial meat processing on both an environmental and a human scale. These arguments may sound convincing, but they obscure a host of problems that result when urban backyards are transformed into slaughterhouses.

The most obvious concern relates to quality of life. Not every urban dweller wants to live next door to a stable of farm animals. In Oakland, Calif., one resident whose home abuts a backyard farm housing dozens of animals was recently kept up all night by the moaning of a dying goat (who had eaten poison accidentally left out by the "farmer").

A father snapped the head off a chicken with a pair of garden shears in full view of his very young son, whom his other son, a blogger, proudly deemed "a chicken murderer in training."

Neighbors eventually filed a complaint against this farm, citing (among other issues), "increased noise, flies, [and] odor." In another incident, the Los Angeles County Animal Control, with the help of a nonprofit called the Gentle Barn, rescued more than 50 animals about to be slaughtered by a "Southern California backyard butcher" who was routinely abusing his animals. Not only were all his creatures emaciated, but they had "infected lungs, parasites, fevers, and hacking coughs." Last summer, backyard chickens and ducks infected more than 71 people with two separate strains of salmonella. Urban centers already deal with plenty of daunting health and safety issues. Do we really want to add traditionally rural ones to the mix?

Another problem has to do with dedication and experience. As Herrick Kimball, the Deliberate Agrarian, consistently notes, animal husbandry is a life-consuming project requiring considerable resources. However, if articles like "A Hipster's

Guide to Farm Animals" are any indication, this newer demographic may have commitment issues. Geared toward Phoenix residents thinking about "jumping the hipster bandwagon and getting a farm animal," this twee manual instructs potential chicken owners to "prepare yourself to be stunned by how cool [chickens] are," adding, "imagine it's like dating a funky hipster chick—no matter how hard you try, you won't be as cool as that sexy-ass chick."

This hipster-speak seems to characterize a lot of urban chicken writing. A first-person piece published in Canada's *Globe and Mail* recounts the experience of an architect who, after deciding to raise chickens, declares that "the Ladies [his chicks], pea-sized brain and all" truly appreciate his chicken-rearing efforts—efforts that enabled him to achieve "hipster status at last, after all these years." This quest for hipster-farmer bona fides has even led chicken coop manufacturers to capitalize on the movement: Witness the Nogg, a $2,800 chicken coop designed to resemble a huge cedar egg, which some have dubbed a "chicken coop for hipster chicken." But the "Hipster's Guide" is the ultimate source for flippant comments minimizing the gravity of owning farm animals. It notes that while backyard eggs might not be an aphrodisiac, what's sure to provide sexual enthrallment is "telling that babe or dude whom you found sleeping next to you . . . that you have farm fresh eggs to shove in their face hole." As for keeping pigs, the manual informs our young hipsters how "pigs are crazy smart" and "LOUD." The authorities on this chicken and pig advice are, respectively, the author of a dating column and the owner of a tattoo parlor.

Hipster questing notwithstanding, backyard butchers commonly claim that an important benefit of raising and slaughtering their own animals is that doing so fosters a sense of dignity for the animals who "gave" their lives for our culinary pursuits. Mark Zuckerberg sang this tune last year when he publicly vowed to personally slaughter all the meat he ate, explaining that it would make him more "thankful" for his food. The claim that DIY slaughter promotes respect for animal welfare seems sensible enough, but it's routinely belied by backyard butchers who blog. What they publish suggests that killing animals is as likely to desensitize as it is to nurture empathy for our non-human friends.

> *One hopes that, as cities rush to revise their codes, they will realize that the gruesome job of killing dinner . . . is better left to deliberate rural agrarians than fickle urbanites whose hipster cred matters a lot more to them than the animals they keep.*

Examples are all too easy to find. An urban farmer in Austin, Texas, had this immediate reaction after improperly slaughtering a duck and watching it thrash blood all over her yard for 10 minutes: "Good thing I wore old pants and sneakers." A man who killed his own turkey concluded, "the thrill of killing your own food is an exhilaration better than skydiving." He was especially pleased to discover how "there is something so pure and animalistic about it." (His blog is now defunct.) In another case, a father snapped the head off a chicken with a pair of garden shears in full view of his very young son, whom his other son, a blogger, proudly deemed "a chicken murderer in training." Training, though, is often exactly what's missing among DIY butchers. As Karen Davis, president of the animal-welfare group United Poultry Concerns, told me in an email, "Most amateur slaughterers don't know a carotid artery from a jugular vein." (In a piece about the Foxfire books in *Slate* earlier this year, Britt Peterson uncovered some examples of amateur-slaughter disaster stemming from this kind of ignorance.)

A final observation about urban husbandry is that, paradoxically, it fails to confront one of the biggest problems with industrial agriculture: It doesn't provide animals sufficient space to behave naturally. This limitation is illuminated by the urban farm permit approved last April [2012] by the city of Oakland for Novella Carpenter, author of the book *Farm City* and a maven of urban farming.

According to Carpenter's Minor Conditional Use Permit for her 4,500-square-foot urban residential plot, her farm is allowed to keep more than 40 animals, including ducks, chickens, rabbits, pigs, and goats. While 100 square feet per animal is certainly generous by industry standards, it pays no heed to the fact that, under natural conditions, these animals would cover miles of diverse landscape, including open pastures. Carpenter's permit actually requires that the animals be constantly confined to prevent their manure from contaminating the crops being grown on the premises. When pressed on the issue of raising farm animals in the city, Carpenter suggested that animal welfare was hardly her top concern. She told Bloomberg *Businessweek*, "[W]e just want to kill a chicken."

Carpenter is not alone in this sentiment. Urbanites are increasingly seeking the right to slaughter at home. However, in a hopeful turn of events, Carpenter's permit contains this unexpected stipulation: "NO onsite animal slaughtering/ butchering." One hopes that, as cities rush to revise their codes, they will realize that the gruesome job of killing dinner—if it has to be done—is better left to deliberate rural agrarians than fickle urbanites whose hipster cred matters a lot more to them than the animals they keep.

6

Backyard Animal Slaughter Should Be Permitted

Kiera Butler

Kiera Butler writes the weekly "Econundrums" column for Mother Jones *magazine, where she is a senior editor.*

Many of the criticisms that are voiced about backyard animal raising and slaughter are not supported by the facts. Critics maintain that backyard husbandry leads to more animals being abandoned at animal shelters; that it has a negative effect on children; that it lowers property values; that urban farming means raising plants, not animals; and that animal agriculture in urban areas is an elitist practice that does nothing to address the real issues of food security and inequality in American society. None of these assertions are supported by facts, however. Backyard animal slaughter should be permitted because allowing people access to fresh meat that is not produced by the industrial factory-farm system is a healthy thing for people and communities.

A few weeks ago, my friend was handed a flier at a farmers market in Oakland, California. It's from a local group called Neighbors Opposed to Backyard Slaughter [NOBS] that wants the City of Oakland to forbid people to raise livestock on their property. Around here, urban farming is a pretty hot issue; a nonprofit called City Slicker Farms has been promoting DIY [do-it-yourself] food production for several years, and author and farmer (and *Mother Jones* contributor) Novella Carpenter brought the practice into the limelight with her 2009 book *Farm City: The Education of an Urban Farmer*, about her experiences at her Oakland farm.

Now I'm obviously biased on this issue; I've written on this site about the experience of raising turkeys for meat in my Berkeley backyard. But when I read through the anti-urban farming arguments put forth on the flier, I couldn't resist making a rebuttal. Herewith, some sections of the flier, along with my responses. First up:

More Abandoned Animals?

The Oakland Animal Shelter is already underfunded and over-whelmed with abandoned dogs & cats. They don't have the re-sources to take in farmed rabbits, hens, and goats. More animals dumped at the shelter means more dogs & cats euthanized.

I'm not the only one who thinks that kids learn from raising and processing animals. The 4-H Club has been doing it for a century.

I called the Oakland Animal Shelter and asked whether it had seen an uptick in livestock (chickens, rabbits, and goats) since the urban farming trend took off around 2005. While the number of chickens at the shelter has gone up in recent years, from 213 in 2009 to 340 in 2010, shelter director Megan Webb attributes that increase to the city's crackdown on fighting roosters in 2010, when the city confiscated hundreds of roosters. Aside from that, said Webb, "I've asked several of my animal control officers and they don't feel like we have been seeing more livestock-type animals in the field or being impounded in the shelter."

Negative Impact on Children?

The last thing I want my daughter to see or hear are the sounds of an animal being killed next door by a DIY slaughter hobbyist.

Obviously, this one's a matter of personal parenting choice. But one thing I do know: Kids are very curious about where their food comes from. I witnessed this curiosity firsthand when a bunch of neighborhood rapscallions showed up for the slaughter of one of my turkeys. I'm not sure how they even knew about it. Word must have gotten around. Sure, there were giggles and morbid jokes aplenty. But I'm pretty certain that the kids got something valuable out of the experience, too. I talked to a little girl who had never seen a turkey up close before. A few others wanted to get right up close to the processing to see what it was all about. I'm not the only one who thinks that kids learn from raising and processing animals. The 4-H Club has been doing it for a century.

Lower Property Values?

People who want to start a business or buy a house in Oakland will be deterred by the sounds and smell of farmed animals on the neighboring property.

I wanted to see whether local real estate agents saw neighbors with livestock as a deterrent for potential home buyers, so I called up Elisa Uribe at Wells & Bennett Realtors, which sells homes in Oakland. "Keeping animals in the yard certainly does seem to be the trend, and I have not heard of it as a deterrent at all," she said. "I actually have a rental property where the neighbors have three or four chickens. We've had a variety of different tenants and they've never complained. I don't think that having neighbors with animals would lower property values at all."

Why Not Plants Only?

I absolutely support urban agriculture, but doesn't that mean plants? We need to increase access to healthful foods, which means fruits and vegetables.

Now this one just strikes me as silly. I don't know anyone who is raising animals instead of gardening; most urban farmers are doing both. In fact, urban farming groups convinced Oakland to change its rules so that people could sell crops from their garden out of their homes. Pitting animal-raising against vegetable-raising is a strange and nonsensical rhetorical strategy.

And one more from Neighbors Opposed to Backyard Slaughter's website:

Introducing animal agriculture into Oakland's food policy would be an unjust distribution of resources because it would serve the needs of a small group of people interested in creating artisan animal products instead of serving the low-income communities that the city of Oakland mandated the Planning Department to create food policy to serve.

Essentially, NOBS is arguing that allowing people to raise their own meat would be elitist, since everyone who raises animals is a foodie who wants to host heritage omelet brunches. That's blatantly untrue. What about immigrants who come from places where tending animals is a way of life? And why shouldn't people in the "low-income communities" get to produce their own eggs, which would likely be cheaper and healthier than eggs from the supermarket?

Charting a Future Course

Local rules about urban farming vary widely. Oakland is currently in the process of revising its urban agriculture policy. Oakland Food Policy Council coordinator Esperanza Pallana told me that under current rules, residents who obtain a home occupation permit are allowed to sell plant-based crops and raw agricultural products—which includes eggs and honey, but not meat. Urban farming advocates are now in the process of trying to make it easier for urban farmers to raise their own meat. Meanwhile, in the neighboring community of El Cerrito, the city attorney ruled last November in favor of letting people raise and process animals on their property, arguing that forbidding such a practice could be a violation of

First Amendment rights (for example, the rights of people who want to slaughter animals according to halal rules).

I could go on. And perhaps in some other post, I will. For now, though, I'll leave it at this: My colleague Tom Philpott writes regularly about the deplorable practices of factory farms and the growing body of evidence that the meat that they produce is not healthy. To my mind, any rule that provides an alternative to mass-produced animal products would be a step in the right direction.

7

Cities Weigh Rules for Urban Beekeeping

Patricia E. Salkin

Patricia E. Salkin is the Raymond and Ella Smith Distinguished Professor of Law and the associate dean and director of the Government Law Center at Albany Law School in New York.

Backyard beekeeping has grown in popularity in recent years as part of the burgeoning urban farming movement. Urban bees pollinate local flowers and trees, produce honey for the local economy, and help offset a dire honeybee health crisis that has recently swept through the commercial beekeeping industry. Beekeeping activities have typically been regulated by the states, but as small-scale apiarists set up in residential areas, cities nationwide are discovering that their states' regulations are not very applicable. While some cities ban backyard beekeeping entirely, others are working to create policies to regulate the practice. Typical rules may limit the number of hives and where they can be placed in relation to neighbors' properties; establish requirements for water availability, fire safety, and "flyway" barriers; and even require beekeeper registration with the city.

U rban beekeeping, along with other types of sustainable development and green building, has generated quite a buzz in recent years. Since 2009, the White House has maintained a hive of 70,000 bees that produce honey for the presi-

Patricia E. Salkin, "Honey, It's All the Buzz: Regulating Neighborhood Bee Hives," *Boston College Environmental Affairs Law Review*, vol. 39, Research Paper #19, September 6, 2011. Copyright © 2011 by Boston College Law School. All rights reserved. Reproduced by permission.

dential kitchen and pollinate the vegetables in First Lady Michelle Obama's kitchen garden. Chicago has its own city-managed apiaries at City Hall, in both city zoos, and in the Garfield Park Conservatory. Other cities across the country, including New York, Denver, Milwaukee, and Santa Monica, have recently legalized beekeeping.

Small-scale beekeeping has proven to be especially popular among people looking to obtain more of their food from local sources. Urban bees provide important pollination services to community gardens, home vegetable gardens, and fruit trees. Some people also believe that honey contributes to a healthy lifestyle by providing a minimally-processed sweetener as an alternative to highly manufactured sugar products, such as high-fructose corn syrup, and through its various uses as a homeopathic remedy. Additionally, urban beekeeping may help offset the huge losses that commercial bee populations have suffered since the emergence of colony collapse disorder in 2006.

Small-scale beekeeping bolsters local economies, too. Restaurants benefit by being able to purchase local honey for dishes and cocktails.

Individual states have broad authority to control beekeeping and honey production activities.

Growing Popularity

Further, retail stores are provided with high quality artisanal honeys and beeswax-derived products such as candles, soaps, and cosmetics. Other products, such as pollen, propolis, and royal jelly, can also be harvested and produced from bees and sold as natural remedies or health supplements. The popularity of apiculture and bee products has even led to the establishment of bee-themed festivals and tourism events in some communities, as well as beekeeping and honey-processing classes.

Despite the benefits and growing popularity of backyard beekeeping, apiaries are not always welcomed by the neighbors. This article is designed to provide information to land use regulators about the benefits and drawbacks of beekeeping in residential areas, and to offer strategies for addressing beekeeping activities through local laws and ordinances.

Beekeeping and Honey Regulations

Unlike many other agricultural products, there are relatively few federal restrictions on the production and sale of honey. The U.S. Department of Agriculture (USDA) has the authority to restrict the importation of honeybees and certain honeybee products into or through the United States to protect the beekeeping and honey industries from the introduction and spread of diseases, parasites, and undesirable genetic traits. The USDA also has oversight authority over the National Honey Board, a nonregulatory federal board that conducts research, marketing, and promotional programs. In addition, the USDA considers pollinator protection a high-priority area for their research grants. . . .

Given the limited scope of federal honey regulations, individual states have broad authority to control beekeeping and honey production activities. In most states, apiaries are subject to registration and inspection requirements intended to prevent the spread of bee diseases and parasites. These regulations usually include procedures for conducting inspections, requirements for moving bees into and out of the state, and provisions relating to quarantines, the seizure of infected or noncompliant hives, and the destruction of diseased bees and contaminated equipment. Other bee regulations include requirements for apiary siting and identification, as well as specific provisions for nuisance apiaries and abandoned apiaries. In a few states, hobbyist apiaries are exempt from general bee regulations. . . .

Nuisance Law and Bees

Bees can create a nuisance if they become aggressive or swarm on neighboring property, but they have not typically been considered a per se nuisance. Rather, courts addressing whether hives constitute a nuisance look to injuries resulting from the hive owner's negligence, and the hives' interference with neighbors' enjoyment of their property. In a New York case, for example, a county court determined that while keeping honeybees was generally permissible, the owner still had a "duty of maintaining them in such a manner that they will not annoy, injure or endanger the comfort, repose, health or safety of any considerable number of persons or to render a considerable number of persons insecure in the use of their property. . . ." In a Pennsylvania case, a township claimed that a resident's bees constituted a public nuisance based on neighbors' complaints about brown spots found on laundry that had been hung out to dry. The spots were caused by deposits of the bees' fecal matter and were only produced during the bees' first flight of the spring—when they left the hive heavy with wastes built up over the winter months. The court ruled, based on these facts, that the brown spots were not a frequent enough annoyance to create a nuisance.

> *Beekeeping . . . is usually defined as an agricultural use and may be prohibited in residential areas, and apiaries will be subject to [zoning] requirements for nonconforming uses and accessory structures.*

Conversely, an Ohio court concluded that a defendants' beekeeping and honey business constituted a nuisance based on largely undisputed evidence that after the plaintiffs purchased adjacent land, their property was "invaded by an inordinate number of bees . . . which collect[ed] around their doors and windows, in the grass, and near the farm pond, stinging the plaintiffs and their guests on many occasions. . . ."

Although the defendants argued that liability should be precluded because the plaintiffs came to the nuisance, the court concluded that when the plaintiffs bought their property there was no indication that the premises were subject to any nuisance caused by the bees. Rather, it was only after the plaintiffs purchased their land that the defendants increased the scale of their beekeeping operation, and so it could not be said that the plaintiffs should have foreseen the injuries that would be caused by the defendants' bees.

The location of beehives in relation to adjoining properties is often relevant to the question of nuisance liability. In *Allman v. Rexer*, a Pennsylvania court found that "[i]t is negligence to locate the hives so near a place where persons or animals may be expected to be as to make it appear likely that the bees will be angered by their presence and attack them." Similarly, a Florida court held that a property owner could be found negligent for maintaining beehives so close to neighboring properties as to create a foreseeable risk of injury from bee stings. . . .

Local Beekeeping Regulations

Local governments must be mindful of federal and state regulations in drafting their own bee ordinances, as certain provisions could be subject to preemption. Georgia, for example, expressly precludes a variety of local apiculture regulations:

> No county, municipal corporation, consolidated government, or other political subdivision of this state shall adopt or continue in effect any ordinance, rule, regulation, or resolution prohibiting, impeding, or restricting the establishment or maintenance of honeybees in hives. This Code section shall not be construed to restrict the zoning authority of county or municipal governments.

Agricultural use preemption statutes in some states may also apply to bees and apicultural facilities, as in Illinois, where counties may not ordinarily "impose regulations, eliminate uses, buildings, or structures, or require permits with respect to land used for agricultural purposes, which includes . . . apiculture. . . ." Similarly, local governments in New York are prohibited from unreasonably restricting agricultural activities in certified agricultural districts, and apiaries are specified as falling within this protection.

Where not subject to preemption, apiaries and related land uses will be subject to generally applicable zoning requirements. Beekeeping, for example, is usually defined as an agricultural use and may be prohibited in residential areas, and apiaries will be subject to requirements for nonconforming uses and accessory structures. Some local governments have enacted ordinances specifically pertaining to beekeeping. The following sections discuss common features of these local bee laws.

Some ordinances require beekeepers to install a "flyway barrier," which is usually a solid fence, wall, or dense line of hedges.

Clarifying Rules

Before backyard beekeeping can be permitted, some cities may need to amend their ordinances to clarify that bees are not prohibited wild animals. Last spring, for example, New York City lifted its ban on beekeeping through an amendment to its Health Code that expressly removed nonaggressive honeybees from the list of prohibited "venomous insects." Similarly, Denver bans the keeping of "wild or dangerous animals," but specifically states that domesticated honeybees do not fall within the prohibition. In Littleton, Colorado, beekeeping was recently designated an allowable activity in "park [and] open space" districts.

One of the most common issues addressed in beekeeping ordinances is the number of hives that owners can keep on their property. Minimum lot sizes for beekeeping and colony density regulations help to ensure that urban and suburban apiaries do not grow so large as to create a nuisance. Limiting the number of hives within urban areas may also be important in order to prevent bee populations from outgrowing the supply of available foraging sites.

Beekeeping is permitted in "all or most zoning districts" in Dayton, Ohio, but the city requires a lot size of at least 7500 square feet for the first hive and an additional 5000 square feet for each additional hive. Fort Collins, Colorado, has implemented a similar plan, basing the number of permitted hives on the acreage of the property. Under the regulations, two colonies can be kept on a tract of land that is less than a quarter of an acre. If the parcel is between a quarter and a half-acre, a beekeeper can have up to four colonies. The next size range covers lots ranging from a half to a full acre, and permits up to six colonies on the property. Eight colonies are permitted on any property larger than an acre, but the ordinance includes an exception for additional colonies when they are set back at least two hundred feet from all property lines.

Where Can Hives Be Placed?

Setbacks, like minimum lot size requirements, are commonly used to decrease the potential nuisance effect of beekeeping operations. Setbacks applying to beekeeping activities vary widely in their length and scope. In Dayton, for example, beehives are required to be at least ten feet from any lot line, ten feet from any dwelling, and at least thirty feet from any public sidewalk or roadway. Additionally, Dayton requires the hive's entrance to face "away from the property line of the residential lot closest to the beehive." Larger setbacks are imposed in other cities, as in Tuscaloosa, Alabama, where it is illegal to keep bees within one hundred fifty feet of any school, public park, or playground, or within three hundred feet of any residential property line. San Diego requires that beehives must be located at least one hundred feet from any public roadway.

Flyway Barriers and Water Access

Some ordinances require beekeepers to install a "flyway barrier," which is usually a solid fence, wall, or dense line of hedges. These structures raise the flight path of bees leaving the hive, thereby limiting their interactions with nearby residents. Fort Collins requires six-foot tall flyway barriers spanning ten feet along the property line in both directions, unless the adjoining property is undeveloped for at least twenty-five feet past the property line. Dayton requires that if a hive is within ten feet of a rear or side property line, six-foot fencing must be constructed and must extend at least twenty feet on either side of the hive. The requirement will be waived, however, if the hive is placed on a porch or balcony that is at least ten feet off the ground and at least ten feet from the property line.

It is important for beekeepers to provide water for their bees so that they do not congregate at swimming pools, pet water bowls, birdbaths, and other water sources on neighboring properties. Requirements to this effect have been enacted in New York City and Dayton, Ohio. Beekeeping associations in many other municipalities have proposed similar requirements. While some ordinances include only a general requirement, San Diego's bee ordinance specifies that the water source must be within ten feet of the apiary.

Permits and Other Requirements

Some bee ordinances include registration requirements. In New York City, for example, beekeepers must provide information regarding the number and location of their hives in order to obtain registration from the New York City Department of Health. Local registration requirements might raise preemption issues, however, as many states have enacted comprehensive apiary registration laws.

In San Diego, beekeepers must erect a sign "prominently displayed on the entrance side of the apiary stating, in black letters not less than one inch in height on a background of contrasting color, the name of the owner or person in possession of the apiary, his address, and telephone number." Fort Collins also requires that apiary owners "conspicuously post" signs with their name and contact information. Other cities have enacted similar requirements.

Fire Safety Regulations

When harvesting honey, beekeepers typically fill the hives with smoke to subdue the bees. Cities may impose restrictions on smokers because they create an obvious fire hazard. San Diego, for example, requires the apiary controller to maintain a firebreak at least thirty feet wide in all directions around the apiary. Within this firebreak, the first ten feet from the apiary must be kept free of combustible material and any vegetation must be six inches or shorter. Vegetation up to a foot tall is permitted in the remaining twenty feet. San Diego also requires the apiary controller to maintain basic fire-fighting materials, such as shovels, fire extinguishers, and hoses. Additionally, the bee smoker must be completely extinguished by water prior to transportation, or it must be placed in a securely fastened metal container.

Balancing Both Sides

Designing effective beekeeping ordinances requires local governments to address concerns about nuisances, but they must also be aware of beekeepers' complaints that local regulations are too strict and that state laws, general zoning requirements, and nuisance liability are sufficient to ensure the safe and sanitary operation of beehives. When the proper balance is struck between these competing interests, beekeeping ordinances can become an important part of a city's urban agriculture regulations.

8

"Guerrilla Gardeners" Spread Seeds of Social Change

Emily Wax

Emily Wax is a national staff writer for The Washington Post, *where she has worked in various capacities since 1999.*

A more political and activist-oriented aspect of urban farming is the phenomenon known as "guerrilla gardening," in which people raise crops or plant trees and flowers on abandoned properties or on publicly owned land, such as freeway margins. Advocates say that claiming unused urban land and transforming it via gardening not only beautifies formerly blighted urban spaces but advances issues of social justice by increasing community access to fresh produce, especially in inner-city neighborhoods. Police, meanwhile, say that guerrilla gardening is illegal, and others have concerns about the safety of people consuming foods that have been grown near freeways and in industrial areas where the soil may be toxic from prior uses of the property. Although activist gardening mainly takes place in cities, suburban strip malls and parking lots also see attention from guerrilla gardeners.

"Let's throw some bombs," a young woman calls out, waterproof floral purse swinging on her shoulder and Laura Ingalls braids flying behind her as a band of 25 followers cheer, "Cool!"

They rush toward a drab vacant lot in Shaw. Some climb up onto the back of a truck to get better aim at their target. But these bombers aren't likely to appear on any terrorist list or even get arrested. They're throwing "seed bombs," golf-ball-size lumps of mud packed with wildflower seeds, clay and a little bit of compost and water, which they just learned to make at a free seed-bombing workshop for Washington's guerrilla gardeners.

The benign bombing is part of a larger phenomenon known as activist gardening that is taking off this spring in cities such as Portland, Detroit, Baltimore and the District, where young urbanites are redefining the seemingly fusty pastime as a tool for social change. This is civil disobedience with a twist: Vegetable patches and sunflower gardens planted on decrepit medians and in derelict lots in an effort to beautify inner-city eyesores or grow healthful food in neighborhoods with limited access to fresh food.

Radical Food Justice

"Guerrilla gardening is urban gardening and food justice. It's just this really cool mix," says Emmy Gran, 25, who is teaching seed-bombing in a floppy sun hat at a recent Saturday morning workshop in the courtyard of Old City Green, a gardening store in Shaw. "But it's controversial, too. If you see an abandoned, neglected lot and you decide to do something about it by planting vegetables and herbs, are you an occupier? It's kind of radical, in some ways."

And every radical movement needs graffiti. Gran hauls out her Cuisinart to make the green "spray-paint" required for gardening activism's biodegradable moss graffiti. Ingredients: moss, a half teaspoon of sugar and beer or yogurt which, when blended, will stick to walls. ("You can also use buttermilk," she adds.) With a light rain starting to fall, the group walks over to a curb near the garden store and uses the gloppy mixture to write "Nourish, Grow, Shaw" in big, moss-green letters.

[Guerrilla gardening] has spread in the United States in recent years, spurred by the "green" movement and the increased demand for locally grown, healthful food.

Activist gardening is the latest face of social justice in the District. Forget living in a tent in McPherson Square. Instead, try pulling on muddy work boots and hauling fertilizer and mulch to a forlorn lot, then persuading your housemates to get off their iPads and go outdoors to plant snap peas and garlic. The group at the workshop includes former Peace Corps volunteers, environmental activists, plaid-ensconced hipsters and social justice workers, all eager to learn more about subversive or sneaky gardening, as it is also known.

"It's all a lot less devious than it seems," says Ellen Abramowitz, 22, who works for the Alliance to Save Energy, a nonprofit group that educates schools about energy efficiency. "Besides, who doesn't love flowers?"

One Flower at a Time

Gran tells her students—most of whom were born in the 1980s—that guerrilla gardening dates from the late-1960s establishment of People's Park in Berkeley, Calif., when a disused patch of land near the University of California campus was co-opted by the community and reimagined as a public green. Today, she says, it takes place in more than 30 countries, with much of the activity documented on the British-based Web site guerrillagardening.org. It has spread in the United States in recent years, spurred by the "green" movement and the increased demand for locally grown, healthful food.

"I think it's also a democratic statement and an experiment in re-creating space," says Columbia Heights environmental consultant Tristanne Days, 24, as she carefully assembles seed bombs. "We're making the city what we want."

They're doing it one flower at a time. The bombs will—in theory—bloom into bachelor's buttons and baby's breath, forget-me-nots and marigolds when the truffle-size balls hit, then expand. It also helps if there's a healthy spring rain, said Scott Aker, head of horticulture for the U.S. National Arboretum. If the bombs are launched into a sunny space where there's not too much other vegetation present, then he gives the seeds a 70 percent chance of blooming. "But either way, it sounds like great fun," Aker says. "On your commute, you can toss one out the window."

District police say that guerrilla gardening technically constitutes unlawful entry, a misdemeanor. But, says D.C. police spokeswoman Gwendolyn Crump, "nothing like this has come to our attention." Although there have been reports of gardens being bulldozed to make way for development, gardeners say the issue of small-scale gardening is typically hashed out between property owners and the people doing the planting.

Permits for Planting

Not everyone at Gran's workshop is a guerrilla gardener. Some of the young people attending the class—run by Knowledge Commons D.C., an organization that provides free public workshops on a variety of subjects—have secured permits for their plots.

This spring Sarah McLaughlin, 25, and her boyfriend Josh Singer, 31, started a community "parken" on a 2.7-acre parcel of unused land north of Howard University. They named it Wangari Gardens after Wangari Maathai, the Nobel Prize-winning Kenyan environmental activist. (Although it took months, Singer was able to obtain a public-use permit from the Department of Transportation, which oversees the land, to garden there.)

"We're a real D.C. love story," McLaughlin says with a laugh as Singer puts his soil-stained arm around her after a long day of gardening. The couple fell in love at the Occupy D.C. camp in McPherson Square, where they were both living this past fall. Singer works for D.C.-based nonprofit group Casey Trees, which helps local schools and urban communities plant trees. McLaughlin is a manager for Old City Green and teaches an after-school garden and nutrition program at D.C. Prep Public Charter School in Northeast.

"We saw the land near where we have a group house, and we wanted to use green space to build community," says Singer, who's wearing an "I Dig Trees" T-shirt under his Carhartt jacket. So far, McLaughlin and Singer have helped the community plant 59 garden plots in Wangari Gardens, each tended by neighbors who live nearby and pay annual dues to grow food and flowers in a raised garden bed with advice from experienced gardeners. (On a recent visit to Wangari, several longtime residents said they were happy with the garden because the land had been vacant for so long.)

Go to sleep one night and wake up, and there's corn growing in the derelict lot by your check-cashing store.

Singer has put $3,000 in soil and other supplies on his credit card. But he hopes the garden will flourish and that he will eventually obtain sufficient funding and grants to add a dog park, a butterfly/native plant garden and an outdoor classroom. On Sunday [April 15, 2012], Wangari will host a Repurposing Space Day to showcase ways that local organizations can reuse vacant or underutilized land in the District.

"There's just so many really cool gardening projects going on around Washington," Singer says. "It's a great moment."

An Urban Phenomenon

During Wangari's creation, the pair sought advice from Dennis Chestnut, 63, whom they see as the father of the District's activist gardening scene. He is founder and executive director of Groundwork Anacostia River D.C., a nonprofit group that seeks to reclaim vacant and neglected land for conservation, recreation and economic development. He helped start two community vegetable gardens in wards 7 and 8, "in places where convenience stores typically sell alcohol and chips," he said.

Chestnut says he's proud that the young people in Washington are suddenly so interested in gardening. "Go to sleep one night and wake up, and there's corn growing in the derelict lot by your check-cashing store," he laughs. "I'm all for all of it: guerrilla gardening, community gardens. These young people living in D.C. are just go-getters. But I'm also a child of the '60s. I understand it's really important to organize all of us so we can work on common issues."

There's so much new community gardening going on in the District, he says, that it's tough to keep track. Some takes place under the auspices of nonprofit organizations. City Blossoms works with D.C. public school students to beautify city spaces and grow, harvest and prepare vegetables; the Common Good City Farm is an education center that teaches low-income residents how to grow their own healthful food. More often, though, activist gardening is undertaken by friends or neighbors who seed-bomb potholes or trash-strewn lots.

Planting in Suburbia

Although activist gardening is largely an urban phenomenon, there are self-described "suburban guerrilla gardeners" in Arlington County and Alexandria, Wheaton and Gaithersburg who have organized meet-ups online. They describe stealthily turning empty spaces that abut strip malls, highways and parking lots into verdant flower and herb gardens. Eco City

Farm in Edmonston has a trainee program that teaches immigrants urban farming—from composting to harvesting to marketing—so they can sell produce to farmers markets. Gran, who lives in Olney, says she recently engaged in clandestine wildflower-planting along a number of country roads.

When you live in the city and you see a space that's yucky, you can make it more beautiful.

Chestnut is working with City Council member Tommy Wells (D-Ward 6), who wants the city to develop a permit process for community gardening and provide an inventory of vacant District land that could be used for community gardens. He also hopes to provide the gardens with better access to water. "I see guerrilla gardening more as a byproduct of a city that can't provide the support and assistance to residents that want to establish community gardens," Wells said. "The city shouldn't make it this hard."

Not Everyone Approves

Not everyone shares Wells's enthusiasm. A recent forum on the neighborhood blog Prince of Petworth prompted responses from posters who warned that vegetables grown near roads with heavy traffic could be toxic. Others wrote that guerrilla gardening—which sits at the nexus of gentrification and environmentalism—was an example of overly exuberant gentrifiers hoping to take over neighborhoods that may not want to change.

But the young people at Gran's workshop say guerrilla gardening is making Washington a more progressive city. They gather after the workshop and talk about planning an outing on May 1, which has been declared International Sunflower Guerrilla Gardening Day online by a group of gardeners in Brussels that wants people all over the world to engage in the possibly illegal act of planting sunflowers on neglected land.

Guerrilla gardeners say every day is sunflower-planting day. "When you live in the city and you see a space that's yucky, you can make it more beautiful," says Theresa Blaner, 33, who writes the blog D.C. Guerilla Gardeners. Like most guerrilla gardeners, she's never been arrested for it.

"But it would be *awesome* to have a [police] record for gardening," she laughs.

9

Urban Farming Benefits the Local Economy

Adrianne Pasquarelli

Adrianne Pasquarelli is a reporter at Crain's New York Business.

Urban agriculture is no longer just a hobby for many people; it has grown into a viable business model that can serve big-name retail clients, such as Whole Foods. Growing food in the city means it is closer to where it is consumed, so it stays fresh longer and generates less loss for the businesses that use or sell it. Urban gardening operations train and employ local people, generate local tax revenue, supply local stores and restaurants, and encourage the consumption of local products—all of which are good for the local economy. Many cities, and New York in particular, are investing in the future of urban agriculture by helping farm entrepreneurs finance and find space for their projects because they recognize that it will benefit the city economically.

When Whole Foods debuts its long-awaited Brooklyn location in the Gowanus neighborhood this year [2013], it will boast another first—a commercial-scale rooftop farm. The 20,000-square-foot greenhouse facility, operated by local grower Gotham Greens, will produce the Butterhead lettuce, tomatoes and herbs that consumers will find downstairs in the vegetable aisle.

Adrianne Pasquarelli, "Gotham Farmers Sprout Cash Crops," CrainsNewYork.com, July 28, 2013. Reprinted with permission, Crain's New York Business July 28, 2013. © Crain Communications, Inc.

"Our climate-controlled greenhouse can grow 365 days of the year," said Gotham Greens Chief Executive Viraj Puri, noting that the produce from the company's existing Greenpoint, Brooklyn, facility sells at more than 30 local establishments— most of them supermarkets. "We can do the volume and consistency and reliability that big chains require."

In a mere few years, urban agriculture has moved beyond its offbeat roots into a viable business model, attractive to grocers from Whole Foods to A&P. Early city-farming pioneers such as Gotham Greens, which began three years ago, and Brooklyn Grange Farm, another three-year-old venture, are busy expanding their chard and spinach operations by the acre, while the city is reviewing proposals for a farm at Hunts Point in the Bronx.

Urban agriculture has been around for centuries. . . . In the past few years, however, the movement has skyrocketed in popularity and become a more corporate affair.

Seed Money

Meanwhile, city and state governments are recognizing the industry for its potential to improve the environment and create jobs—and are providing the seed money to help it grow. The New York City Department of Environmental Protection and New York State Energy, Research & Development Authority [NYSERDA] have both awarded grants to urban farms for expansion, and in June, the city's Housing Authority established a one-acre farm at a housing project in Red Hook, Brooklyn. Restaurants are also joining the fray, launching operations literally from the ground up.

"Cities are beginning to realize urban agriculture is much more than growing tomatoes and kale," said Nevin Cohen, assistant professor of environmental studies at the New School.

"It's beneficial as an ecological business and for the social benefits that accrue from growing food in the city."

Of course, maintaining a farm in the city isn't as easy as planting seedlings in the dirt, and not all ventures are profitable. The cost of starting a greenhouse to produce fresh produce year-round can be enormous. BrightFarms, which finances, builds and operates such ventures, is spending about $4 million to construct a 100,000-square-foot hydroponic greenhouse on a roof in Sunset Park, Brooklyn, that is scheduled to open early next year.

Fortunately for the Manhattan-based company, which started as a nonprofit in 2006 before evolving into a farm operator working with supermarkets a few years ago, it has raised $13 million in financing from investors including NGEN Partners and Emil Capital Partners. The company, which is focused on growth and on rolling out projects nationwide, is not yet profitable, said Chief Executive Paul Lightfoot. Though the venture-capital community is betting on his firm, other startups might not have as much luck.

"The expenses are huge," said Michael Levenston, who runs City Farmer, a Vancouver, Canada-based site focused on urban agriculture. "That is the million-dollar question for everybody right now: Are you going to survive as a business?"

A Booming Industry

Urban agriculture has been around for centuries, gaining steam with residents in New York City during the Depression and waning in the mid-20th century as city dwellers decamped for the suburbs.

In the past few years, however, the movement has skyrocketed in popularity and become a more corporate affair. After the recession, laid-off workers and college graduates looking for new and innovative jobs turned to the industry as a way to capitalize on the locavore food movement, which has also seen a steady rise.

"In the past four to five years, there has been huge growth, particularly in New York," said Mr. Cohen.

Meanwhile, real estate opportunities are ripe for the picking. There are nearly 5,000 acres of vacant land in New York City suitable for farming—the equivalent of six times the area of Central Park—as well as 1,000 acres of Housing Authority and park space, according to a recent study conducted by Columbia University's Urban Design Lab. The study estimated there are roughly another 4,000 acres of potentially usable rooftop space.

In addition to its career-development potential, urban farming offers valuable infrastructure remedies, as local governments are discovering.

Indeed, the city is taking advantage. In addition to the Red Hook farm, four other farms are planned to launch on Housing Authority property by next summer. The Red Hook project, where collards, kale, broccoli and blueberries are now planted, is designed to provide 18- to 24-year-olds with new skills for the workforce.

"The farm itself is a training farm designed to help engage young men and women in agricultural activities and help them line up careers in urban agriculture," explained Ian Marvy, executive director of Added Value, a nonprofit partner on the project.

Infrastructure Improvements

In addition to its career-development potential, urban farming offers valuable infrastructure remedies, as local governments are discovering.

Two years ago, the city invested $600,000 to expand Brooklyn Grange beyond its Long Island City, Queens, farm into the Brooklyn Navy Yard, as part of its green infrastructure plan. Located on the roof, the farm, which was founded by industrial engineer Ben Flanner, captures storm water, slowing down flooding on the ground level. This winter, Brooklyn Grange will construct a business incubator and a building for the homeless in the South Bronx in conjunction with the South Bronx Overall Economic Development Corp. Both projects will include green roofs with gardens.

"They will make an important environmental impact in terms of air-quality improvement and storm-water retention," said Gwen Schantz, Brooklyn Grange's chief operating officer.

Similarly, Gotham Greens, which Mr. Puri said is profitable, is partly financed by a $400,000 grant from NYSERDA. Mr. Puri declined to provide revenue figures.

These ventures also provide commercial supermarkets with valuable marketing potential. Whole Foods, for example, labels its Gotham Greens with large "local" stickers. Though the packages of lettuce are priced a penny more than organic brands grown farther away, consumers are still clamoring to buy them, especially since their shelf life exceeds that of the competition, said a spokesman for the Austin, Texas-based supermarket chain.

Restaurants Keep It Local

"It doesn't have to be trucked thousands of miles from around the country like some other items," he said. "There are a lot of reasons why it's ideal."

The Gowanus store is expected to open in late fall. If the model proves successful, it will be repeated at other locations.

If we go to this much trouble to grow our eggplant, it sends a message that we pretty much care about everything we do.

Restaurants also see the potential in local growing. Italian eatery Rosemary's opened last year on the Lower East Side with a garden upstairs for its produce. Riverpark, the Murray

Hill-based restaurant from Tom Colicchio, recently relocated its 10,000-square-foot farm to the plaza next door after work resumed on the stalled construction site where it initially planted roots. Last year, the farm produced more than 5,000 pounds of produce in the summer, and at times 100% of the vegetables on diners' plates come from the farm, said chef Sisha Ortúzar.

Mr. Ortúzar reports a spike in interest not just from visitors, who like to tour the grounds, but also from other restaurants asking how they can start their own farms. Though growing his own doesn't save on food bills, the chef said it does impress diners.

"It shows how much we care about the food," he said. "If we go to this much trouble to grow our eggplant, it sends a message that we pretty much care about everything we do."

Tapping into Local Producers

New York farms are the second-largest growers of apples in the country and the fourth-biggest producers of milk, yet many city supermarkets don't sell local products.

That is slowly changing, however. Several entrepreneurs and nonprofits are working to connect farmers with grocers, chefs and consumers in the city, where there is a huge appetite for all things local. FarmersWeb, Adirondack Grazers Cooperative, Five Acre Farms, City Harvest and GrowNYC are helping farmers get their products into the Big Apple.

"Local farmers were underutilized," said Lisa Sposato, associate director of food sourcing for City Harvest, which supplies food to low-income New Yorkers and purchases below-grade produce from local farmers.

"I had no place to go with my undersized onions," said Chris Pawleski, who owns an onion farm in Goshen, N.Y. City Harvest has bought some 300,000 pounds of onions from him during the past year.

FarmersWeb, which launched about a year ago, connects some 50 farms selling 2,000 different items to restaurants, private schools and corporate dining rooms. The farmers pay a transaction fee, and the buyers pay a delivery service to get the products.

Adirondack Grazers Cooperative in Granville, N.Y., began supplying grass-fed beef on behalf of 14 cattle raisers in Vermont, New York and Massachusetts last September. Started by film producer and farm owner Sarah Teale, the cooperative counts Gramercy Tavern and Ceriello's in Grand Central Terminal Market among its customers. "We realized that what all these farmers needed was marketing and sales help," said Ms. Teale. Ordinarily, beef farmers would get about $1.25 a pound at public auctions, compared with the $3 a pound paid by city customers.

Their product is more expensive than beef from big cattle states Kansas and Texas. "The cooperative's greatest challenge is pricing," Ms. Teale said.

Indeed, the business model for connecting upstate farms with big-city customers is still being tested. In late July, Basis Farm to Chef, a farm-to-table company in Manhattan, filed for Chapter 7 bankruptcy, having run into trouble with the distribution side of the business.

10

Urban Farming Could Help Revitalize Declining Cities

Nina Ignaczak

Detroit-area resident Nina Ignaczak is Watershed Planner at Clinton River Watershed Council in Michigan and project editor at Issue Media Group.

In decline for many years, the city of Detroit currently has some two hundred thousand abandoned properties and vacant lots, a quarter of its total land. Urban farming has boomed in Detroit as a way to revitalize both neighborhoods and the local economy. Until recently though, such efforts were not legally protected because of Michigan's Right-to-Farm statute, which was originally intended to protect rural farmers against complaints from suburban newcomers. In March 2013, the Detroit city council adopted its first urban agriculture zoning ordinance, setting up an exemption to the state law and establishing definitions for urban farm activities. With legal protections in place, Detroit's urban agriculture movement can continue to grow and help revitalize the city.

The City of Detroit, once the wealthiest city in the United States, saw its population peak in 1950 at 1.8 million. In the sixty years since, population declined by 60 percent to approximately 713,000 in 2010.

As a result, the city's once bustling 139-square miles contain an estimated 200,000 vacant parcels comprising a quarter of the city's land area, according to the *Wall Street Journal*. The vacant land stretches for miles, forming vistas across urban prairies interspersed with abandoned structures.

Urban farming has become increasingly popular in recent years as a way to deal with vacant property, revitalize neighborhoods and provide job skills and nutrition to remaining local residents struggling with poverty and a lack of access to fresh produce.

Detroit is no stranger to urban agriculture. The community garden movement in the United States was born in Detroit during the depression of the 1890's, when Detroit mayor Hazen Pingree initiated a program to donate vacant land for gardens to supplement the diets and incomes of the unemployed. These gardens became known as "Pingree's Potato Patches"; the program was subsequently copied by several other large cities.

Detroit's Garden Resource Program, a collaboration between several nonprofits that offers guidance to local gardeners, estimates that there are currently 1400 community, school, and home gardens in Detroit. Many are communal gardens, but the number of non-profit and for-profit urban agriculture business ventures has been steadily increasing in the city.

Progress has been hampered, however, by lack of recognition of urban agriculture as a legitimate land use under city ordinance. Urban farms in the city operated under a veil of uncertainty, with no legal recognition of their right to exist.

The Right-to-Farm Statute

Further complicating matters, Michigan's Right-to-Farm statute, a nuisance law enacted in the early eighties to protect rural farmers against complaints from suburban newcomers, restricts local government regulation of urban agriculture. The statute contains preemptive language preventing local units of government from adopting ordinances more restrictive than the state's, which protects farmers utilizing Generally Accepted Agricultural and Management Practices.

To address this need, the City of Detroit Planning Commission initiated a discovery process in 2009, engaging local farmers and gardeners to develop language for an urban agriculture ordinance that would meet the needs of an urban environment while complying with state law.

A successful business, especially in farming, has to involve planning. How can you plan if it's not exactly legal to do what you want to do?

"We looked at ordinances in other places, to see what made sense for Detroit," Kami Pothukuchi, an urban planning professor at Detroit's Wayne State University, told local NPR-affiliate WDET.

An agreement with the Michigan Agricultural Commission was reached, providing the city an exemption from the state statute. In March 2013, Detroit City Council finally adopted the city's first urban agriculture zoning ordinance recognizing agriculture as a legitimate land use and setting standards for it. Because the ordinance rests on an administrative exemption by the state, courts can possibly test it in the future.

"I think the decision to enact ordinances and legalize farming in the city of Detroit will begin the process of removing barriers for young farmers to create long-term viable businesses," says Alex Bryan, partner in Detroit's Food Field farm and National Young Farmer Coalition board member.

"A successful business, especially in farming, has to involve planning. How can you plan if it's not exactly legal to do what you want to do?" he points out.

What the Ordinance Does

The ordinance establishes legal definitions for an array of urban agriculture uses, including aquaculture, aquaponics, farm stands, farmer's markets, greenhouses, rainwater catchment systems, hoophouses, orchards, tree farms, urban farms and urban gardens. The ordinance operates as an overlay to the city's existing zoning ordinance, specifying the existing zoning classifications allowing urban agriculture by right or conditional use. Site plan requirements and standards are outlined for setback, lighting, maintenance, drainage, nuisance issues, noise and hours of operation. The ordinance grants legal nonconforming use status to all agricultural operations that predate the ordinance.

Production of oats, wheat and rye to maturity is prohibited to avoid rodent problems. The ordinance leaves several issues unaddressed and use of animals in agricultural operations is expressly prohibited. Beekeeping is also not protected under the ordinance.

"Gardeners who keep bees right now . . . are not covered under this ordinance but the city is promising that is coming soon," Pothukuchi told WDET.

"Many issues were not addressed in the ordinance, but [this is] a huge step in the right direction," says Bryan.

"I think for the younger farmers it is encouraging to see a future that is validated and supported by the government," he says.

11

Urban Farming Plays a Crucial Role in Disaster Relief Worldwide

A. Adam-Bradford, Femke Hoekstra, and René van Veenhuizen

A. Adam-Bradford holds an interdisciplinary early career fellowship on urban food production and health risk management at the University of Sheffield in England. Femke Hoekstra is a food systems researcher at Wageningen University in The Netherlands. René van Veenhuizen is senior programme officer for the Resource Centres on Urban Agriculture and Food Security (RUAF Foundation) in The Netherlands.

All around the world, wars, natural disasters, economic collapse, and other emergency events can displace large numbers of people, who are then often forced to live for many years in refugee camps, totally dependent on relief agencies for their survival. Establishing urban agriculture in the aftermath of crisis situations plays an important role in rebuilding communities and moving refugees closer to self-reliance. Besides the immediate benefit of providing fresh food to eat, there are long-term benefits as well, such as generating income for economic independence, strengthening ties with the larger regional community, and contributing to the broader redevelopment of the area. In addition, encouraging urban agriculture activities in a community before *a disaster strikes improves resilience and the community's ability to recover from adversity.*

A. Adam-Bradford, Femke Hoekstra and René van Veenhuizen, "Linking Relief, Rehabilitation and Development: A Role for Urban Agriculture?," *Urban Agriculture Magazine*, no. 21, May 7, 2009. Copyright © RUAF Foundation. All rights reserved. Reproduced by permission.

Natural hazards, civil conflicts, wars and economic crises continue to generate unstable and unsafe conditions, placing immense pressures on communities and local livelihoods. These emergency scenarios often result in people fleeing their homes to other areas or crossing borders to other countries, thereby creating mass refugee situations. Many of these refugees or internally displaced persons (IDPs) have to remain in refugee camps for extended periods or reside (often illegally) in and around urban areas.

Consequently, many people living under the harsh conditions of refugee life will try to improve their food security by establishing some form of agriculture, such as small-scale gardening in refugee camps, in backyards, or on open spaces outside settlements. And where land is limited they may resort to micro-technologies, such as container gardening, pots on shelves or hanging baskets. . . .

Different types of hazards can cause disasters or trigger crisis situations. Disasters can be rapid-onset or slow-onset, the latter building up over a period of months. If the crisis is characterised by political instability or high levels of violence, it is often referred to as a complex emergency. . . .

Economic Upheaval

Economic crises result in rising food prices, declining real wages, formal labour market redundancies, and cuts in food subsidies. Reduced public expenditure also has its impact on basic services and infrastructure. In these situations refugees, migrants and the urban poor frequently resort to nonmarket (informal sector) livelihood activities, including urban agriculture.

Economic crises often have a social or political origin. Probably the best known example of a country adopting a national urban agriculture policy in response to such economic and political constraints is Cuba. Other examples of cities that have promoted backyard gardening, rooftop gardens, institutional and school gardens as a standard component of emergency agricultural response include Harare (Zimbabwe), Lagos (Nigeria), Rosario (Argentina), and Gaza in Palestine.

Whether as a result of a hurricane, prolonged drought, armed conflict or economic crisis, people in disaster situations always experience shortages in their basic needs, such as food, water, shelter and health care.

The current global economic crisis is related to our oil-dependent economy. The price of food, a subsidised commodity for over fifty years, has demonstrated its oil dependency by rising with every dollar on a barrel of oil. But other factors, such as the use of grains for bio fuels and the growing demand for imported food by China and India, have also contributed to steep increases in global food prices. Global food prices have increased 83 percent in the past three years, pushing 100 million people deeper into poverty. It is a sobering fact that cities like London (UK) are never more than five days from food depletion; such is the city's dependence on imported food. Agricultural production in and around cities reduces food transportation costs, and can improve access to (cheaper) fresh food, thus reducing vulnerability in the poorer sections of the city, while also improving the general urban ecology and environment.

Environmental and Natural Disasters

Environmental and natural disasters impact millions of people globally in the form of drought, flooding, hurricanes and earthquakes. According to the International Federation of the Red Cross and Red Crescent Societies the total number of people affected by natural disasters has tripled over the past decade to two billion people, with an average of 211 million people directly affected each year. This is approximately five times the number of people estimated to have been affected by armed conflicts over the past decade. In recent climate change debates it has been said that many cities run the risk of becoming "environmental disaster traps," where a diminished food supply from the rural areas (caused by floods, droughts, gale winds or frost) could lead to severe food shortages.

Human-Caused Crises

Unlike natural disasters, many man-made emergencies are deliberate and intentional acts that cause significant population movements (internal and cross border). These situations involve an intricate web of volatile and often hostile military and political forces. For example, in the Indonesian province of Aceh, conflict, violence and a massive counter-insurgency campaign by the Indonesian military against separatist rebels has displaced more than 300,000 people since 1999. Many of these people were forced to move again after the tsunami of December 2004, which displaced an estimated half-million people—12 percent of the population. The recent crisis in Gaza is another example: the Israeli invasion has caused over 90,000 people to flee their homes, while agricultural life has been thrown into total disarray with the fields, trees and crops destroyed. Most of the agriculture in Gaza can be considered urban, and apart from the aid provided by NGOs [nongovernmental organizations] the rehabilitation of this agriculture is paramount for food security in Gaza.

Whether as a result of a hurricane, prolonged drought, armed conflict or economic crisis, people in disaster situations always experience shortages in their basic needs, such as food, water, shelter and health care. . . .

Food security is one dimension of human security. It relates to availability, access, and use of food. Food *availability* at the household, city or national level can be affected by a war, due to its disruption or destruction of farming land or the transport infrastructure, or by natural disasters such as drought, floods, locust infestations, or mudslides that destroy a harvest. Food *access* at household level can be disrupted by a lack of purchasing power or disease amongst the household members. Food *use* can be affected at an individual level, when people are ill or wounded, or have needs for specific types of food (like pregnant women, young children, people recovering from disease, etc.)

Urban agriculture can play multiple roles in different phases of the disaster management cycle.

The Role of Urban Agriculture

Urban agriculture has always been used as a food security strategy during economic and emergency situations. Examples include the extensive "Dig for Victory" campaign in Britain during the Second World War, and more recently "Operation Feed Yourself" in Ghana during the 1970s. Similarly in many other countries, backyard farming, and institutional and school gardening have all been encouraged during times of food instability. . . .

Directly after a crisis, little attention is given to agricultural production or the protection of farming sites. When relief agencies depart, as they eventually do, outside support and resources decline, often leaving large numbers of affected people dependent on external food aid for extended periods of time.

The reasons to support agriculture-related activities in the early stages of the post-disaster phase are numerous. Firstly, there is a need for fresh and diverse food (in addition to the supply of staple foods). Increasingly the potentials of vegetable gardening and other agricultural production activities (e.g., eggs, mushrooms, medicinal herbs, etc.) in protracted refugee situations are being recognised. Secondly, becoming involved in constructive activities may help people regain dignity, hope and self respect and enhance overall well-being. Home or community gardening activities help increase self-reliance, allowing people to grow their preferred crops and varieties, and can improve their skills and knowledge, while additionally reducing operational costs for humanitarian agencies and potentially contributing to restoring the social fabric of disaster-affected communities. Urban agriculture can play multiple roles in different phases of the disaster management cycle. Instructions for protecting primary food production are given in the Sphere Project guidelines, which also contain planning and design recommendations for allocating small plots of land for use as kitchen gardens.

Long-Term Benefits

In the longer term, gardening also generates income and improves associations and linkages with other refugees or local communities, while contributing to the broader development of the area where refugees are hosted by stimulating local markets and trade.... Finally natural resources can be conserved and protected by promoting sound agricultural practices and introducing waste-recycling systems appropriate to the local conditions.

When developing agriculture-based interventions and projects in urban refugee settings, the following issues should be taken into consideration:

- Physical characteristics of the local setting, such as infrastructure capacities, basic social services (water, sanitation, waste use, health), land availability, energy supply (wood, kerosene)

- Social characteristics, such as IDP / refugee rights, security, social fabric and cohesion (race, tribe, gender), uncertainty, traumas, labour supply (abundant but weakened), and possibility of conflict among refugees and IDPs

- Food availability, food quality, balanced food basket, culture, income, etc.

- Political issues that can inhibit interventions.

In this development process, attention to increased self-reliance is important. Protecting and supporting livelihoods should constitute an early component of an emergency response and can be instrumental in safeguarding food security and minimising relief aid dependency among beneficiaries.

Often stimulated by relief organisations, refugees start growing highly nutritious crops for their own consumption and to address immediate needs.

Livelihood Strategies

The development of livelihood strategies including agriculture and animal husbandry will depend on the availability of, and access to, land, irrigation water, seeds and natural resources, but also freedom of movement. Humanitarian agencies may provide refugees with seeds, tools and when necessary technical support, but access to land and common resources is often constrained by the policies implemented by the host country, which may restrict their freedom and mobility. In particular, access to land is limited by the traditional land tenure system and laws concerning land ownership and rights of usufruct. . . .

Beneficiaries' interest in agricultural activities may evolve over time, as their immediate needs start to be met. But some may not wish to start growing vegetables as this might trigger the impression that they have to settle at that location for an extended period of time. Agriculture for many still has a permanent character. During the first period of emergency relief, agricultural production is unlikely but the planning of future production sites must be taken into account in the camp lay-out or the housing reconstruction plans.

Micro-Technologies

Similarities exist between agriculture in camp settings and in urban and slum areas. Urban agriculture, with its emphasis on space-confined technologies, use of composted organic waste and recycling of grey wastewater, may offer good options for the provision of fresh vegetables, eggs, dairy products and other perishables to the population of the "new town" in ad-dition to generating some income. Often stimulated by relief organisations, refugees start growing highly nutritious crops for their own consumption and to address immediate needs. These crops require only a limited growing period and a low investment, using (often available) traditional knowledge and skills. A number of articles . . . describe the use of low-space technologies that have been developed or propagated in refu-gee camps. These technologies, i.e., the use of (very scarce) lo-cal resources (minimal land of low quality, recycled organic waste and wastewater, local seed, etc.), minimise health and environmental risks.

Resilience

In addition to considering agriculture as an important strat-egy in the transition from relief to rehabilitation and recon-struction, agriculture should be integrated in disaster mitiga-tion strategies, as it contributes to increasing resilience to future disaster impacts. Mitigation is a collective term for all actions taken *prior* to the occurrence of a disaster (pre-disaster measures), including preparedness and long-term risk reduc-tion measures. New insights in the field of disaster risk reduc-tion have demonstrated the essential role of resilience and the strong connection between resilience and the sustainability of socio-ecological systems. Resilience determines the persistence of relationships within a system. Resilience is a measure of a household's, city's or nation's ability to absorb shocks and stresses.

A focus on resilience means emphasising what can be done by a system or a community itself and how to strengthen capacities, notably the:

- Capacity to absorb stress or destructive forces through resistance or adaptation

- Capacity to manage or maintain certain functions and structures during disastrous events

- Capacity to recover or bounce back.

The costs of restoring communities back to something resembling their original states are much greater than the costs of investing in a community disaster risk reduction programme and increasing its resilience before a disaster strikes.

Community gardening helps to build different forms of capital . . . , contributes to longer-term resilience and can reduce the impact of future shocks.

Policy Recommendations

Experiences show that refugee agriculture is not only a survival strategy for displaced people to obtain food on a temporary basis, but it is also a valuable livelihood strategy for those that settle permanently, and for those who eventually return to their home cities or countries. Many displaced people, both in camps and in and around cities, engage in agriculture for subsistence and market production. And more and more local and national authorities, as well as relief agencies, are not only allowing but intentionally supporting agricultural production activities as part of their development strategies. Urban agriculture can play an important role in all aspects of the disaster management cycle and is a multifunctional policy instrument and tool for practical application.

In the post-disaster phase, urban agriculture can contribute to food security through the production of fresh vegetables, thus providing a balanced nutritional input in conjunction with food aid programmes. Often these camps do not have a lot of space available, hence the use of micro-technologies, such as multi-storey gardens. During the recovery period, urban agriculture provides livelihood and income-generating opportunities and contributes to wider social and economic rehabilitation, especially in protracted camps, and in and around cities, where levels of unemployment and urban poverty may be particularly high. Depending on the availability of land, several forms of urban agriculture can be applied in such locations.

Although displaced people have a certain protective status, the reality on the ground often shows that they do not have the right to use land or undertake productive activities. . . . Consequently, the status of refugees and IDPs needs to be improved and implementing agencies need to give adequate attention to human rights and entitlements, such as access to land for gardening and farming.

In addition, community gardening helps to build different forms of capital (social, human, financial, economic, physical, natural, etc.), contributes to longer-term resilience and can reduce the impact of future shocks. To be able to build sustainable, shock-resistant communities, the active engagement of people themselves throughout the process is crucial.

Policies and interventions to promote refugee agriculture need to be included in planning and design at the camp level and should include:

- Adequate camp and slum arrangements

- Promotion of low-space crops and animal production and water saving technologies

- Organisational support and training, both in technology and in reintegration and rehabilitation activities

- Provision of inputs and financial support (which becomes especially important in longer term settings, and when farmers move towards producing for the market) [when] displaced settings want to move from self-consumption to market production.

Increasing Self-Reliance

Income generation from agriculture-based livelihoods will play an increasingly important role in developing economic self-reliance amongst refugee populations, and will help create an effective transition between emergency relief and longer-term development. It is likely that the availability of capital equipment or loan capital for small businesses will improve the ability of displaced people to pursue livelihoods and food security, and it is likely that the benefits will eventually also reach the host community.

Facilitating the change from emergency relief operations towards rehabilitation and sustainable development requires innovations that address current needs, while building and incorporating future perspectives. This requires putting in place participatory mechanisms, such as farmer or gardening groups and farmer field schools. These approaches put farming communities at the centre of the development agenda, thereby strengthening their technical capacities as well as enhancing a sense of community. Multi-stakeholder processes involving public and/or non-government actors can help build governance, which is especially important in fragile states that lack government capacity and willingness to perform key functions and services.

Growing food in camps and cities, when appropriate to the local conditions, reduces dependency on external food supplies, improves the availability and access to more nutritious food, and in the longer term may increase the resilience of people and cities.

Organizations to Contact

The editors have compiled the following list of organizations concerned with the issues debated in this book. The descriptions are derived from materials provided by the organizations. All have publications or information available for interested readers. The list was compiled on the date of publication of the present volume; names, addresses, phone and fax numbers, and e-mail and Internet addresses may change. Be aware that many organizations take several weeks or longer to respond to inquiries, so allow as much time as possible.

Alternative Farming Systems Information Center (AFSIC)
US Department of Agriculture, National Agricultural Library
10301 Baltimore Ave., Room 132, Beltsville, MD   20705-2351
(301) 504-6559 • fax: (301) 504-6927
e-mail: http://afsic.nal.usda.gov/afsic-ask-question
website: http://afsic.nal.usda.gov

The Alternative Farming Systems Information Center (AFSIC) specializes in information related to sustainable and alternative agriculture and livestock farming systems, alternative marketing practices, aquaculture, and small farm issues, among other topics. AFSIC was founded in 1985 and is part of the National Agricultural Library. The "Farms and Community" section of the AFSIC website features comprehensive resources on urban farming, community gardening, and backyard husbandry. A list of AFSIC publications is available on the site and many can be requested in hard copy.

American Community Gardening Association (ACGA)
1777 East Broad St., Columbus, OH   43203-2040
e-mail: info@communitygarden.org
website: www.communitygarden.org

The American Community Gardening Association (ACGA) is a bi-national nonprofit membership organization of professionals, volunteers, and supporters of community greening in urban and rural communities. ACGA and its member organizations work to support all aspects of community food and ornamental gardening, urban forestry, preservation and management of open space, and integrated planning and management of developing urban and rural lands. The organization publishes an e-newsletter and its website includes a national database of community gardens and links to their websites. Publications available from the site include "Growing Communities: How to Build Community Through Community Gardening" and "Cultivating Community: Principles and Practices for Community Gardening as a Community-Building Tool."

BackYard Chickens (BYC)

website: www.backyardchickens.com

BackYard Chickens (BYC) is a community website for individuals interested in backyard chicken-keeping. BYC promotes the green, self-sufficient, and grow-local movements by educating people on how to raise chickens properly. The website hosts active discussion forums for more than one hundred sixty thousand chicken owners who add about six thousand new posts per day. The site also features a "Learning Center" with extensive information, tutorials, articles, and reviews about chickens and chicken-care topics, such as handling, coop-building, slaughter, chicken products, and local laws.

Food and Agriculture Organization of the United Nations (FAO)

Viale delle Terme di Caracalla, Rome   00153
   Italy
(+39) 06 57051 • fax: (+39) 06 570 53152
e-mail: FAO-HQ@fao.org
website: www.fao.org/home/en

The mission of the Food and Agriculture Organization of the United Nations (FAO) is to help communities worldwide achieve food security and make sure people have regular access to enough high-quality food to lead active, healthy lives.

The organization's mandate is to improve nutrition, increase agricultural productivity, raise the standard of living, and contribute to global economic growth. The FAO website features a wide breadth of information about food security issues, as well as resource guides and tutorials on how to establish small-scale agriculture and animal husbandry programs. The site includes a large database of reports and other publications that examine urban food production models worldwide.

Green Guerillas

232 East 11th St., New York, NY   10003
(212) 594-2155
e-mail: info@nycgreen.org
website: www.greenguerillas.org

Founded in 1973, Green Guerillas is a nonprofit organization that has helped hundreds of grassroots groups in New York City use community gardening as a tool to reclaim urban land, stabilize city blocks, and get people working together to solve problems. The group's website features an extensive resource center with information about urban farming, Green Guerilla programs, news items, and numerous links to other similar organizations around the country.

National Gardening Association (NGA)

237 Commerce St., Suite 101, Williston, VT   05495
(802) 863-5251 • fax: (802) 864-6889
website: www.garden.org

The National Gardening Association (NGA) is a Vermont-based national nonprofit focused on garden-based education. Its mission is to empower every generation to lead healthier lives, build stronger communities, and encourage environmental stewardship through educational gardening programs. The organization pursues its mission by providing information and support for youth and school gardening programs, home gardeners, and others—one child, one school, one community at a time. The NGA website includes a special section called

"Kids Gardening," which places a special emphasis on educational school gardens and features extensive resources for and about young people.

Neighbors Opposed to Backyard Slaughter (NOBS)
e-mail: contact@noslaughter.org.
website: http://noslaughter.org

Neighbors Opposed to Backyard Slaughter (NOBS) was created in response to the city of Oakland, California, considering permitting chickens and other animals to be slaughtered by residents at home under its newly revised urban agriculture policy. NOBS supports urban agriculture in general but believes that should be defined as plants only and that backyard husbandry and animal slaughter should be banned. The organization's website features a variety of resources and articles about urban chicken-keeping and slaughter, news updates related to backyard meat and egg production, and the illustrated guide, "How Not to Raise Chickens: A Field Guide for Urban Poultry Farmers."

RUAF Foundation Resource Centres on Urban Agriculture and Food Security
Kastanjelaan 5/ PO Box 64, Leusden   3833 AN
   The Netherlands
(+31) 33 4326039
website: www.ruaf.org

RUAF Foundation Resource Centres on Urban Agriculture and Food Security is an international nongovernmental organization whose mission is to reduce urban poverty and generate employment and food security by empowering urban and semi-urban farmers. RUAF provides training, technical support, and policy advice to local and national governments, producer organizations, nongovernmental organizations, and other stakeholders. The RUAF website contains news archives, videos, and an extensive online bibliographic database related to urban farming topics. Its *Urban Agriculture Magazine* is archived on the site and is available in seven languages. Among the many other publications available on the group's website are the reports "Cities Farming for the Future," "Cities, Food and Agriculture," and "Women Feeding Cities."

United Poultry Concerns

PO Box 150, Machipongo, VA   23405
(757) 678-7875 • fax: (757) 678-5070
e-mail: info@upc-online.org
website: www.upc-online.org

United Poultry Concerns is a nonprofit organization dedicated to the compassionate and respectful treatment of chickens, turkeys, ducks, and other domestic fowl. The group works to make the public aware of the ways in which poultry are used and to promote the benefits of a vegan diet and lifestyle. The organization publishes a quarterly magazine, *Poultry Press*, and its website includes a section dedicated to the issues surrounding urban chicken-keeping.

Urban Farming

19785 W. 12 Mile #537, Southfield, MI   48076
(313) 664-0615
e-mail: www.urbanfarming.org/contact.html
website: www.urbanfarming.org

Urban Farming is a nonprofit that started in Detroit in 2005 and then grew into a global organization that encourages and supports community gardeners worldwide. There are currently more than sixty-one thousand gardens registered with Urban Farming as part of a global food chain in more than twenty countries around the world. The organization's website features information about Urban Farming's various programs, a library of urban agriculture educational videos, news updates, a garden locator, and opportunities to get involved with the group's projects.

Bibliography

Books

Novella Carpenter *Farm City: The Education of an Urban Farmer.* New York: Penguin, 2009.

Novella Carpenter and Willow Rosenthal *The Essential Urban Farmer.* New York: Penguin, 2011.

Jennifer Cockrall-King *Food and the City: Urban Agriculture and the New Food Revolution.* New York: Prometheus, 2012.

Temra Costa *Farmer Jane: Women Changing the Way We Eat.* Layton, UT: Gibbs Smith, 2010.

Amy Franceschini *Farm Together Now.* San Francicso: Chronicle Books, 2010.

Katherine Gustafson *Change Comes to Dinner: How Vertical Farmers, Urban Growers, and Other Innovators Are Revolutionizing How America Eats.* New York: St. Martin's Griffin, 2012.

David Hanson and Edwin Marty *Breaking Through Concrete: Building an Urban Farm Revival.* Berkeley: University of California Press, 2012.

Peter Ladner *The Urban Food Revolution: Changing the Way We Feed Cities.* Gabriola Island, BC: New Society, 2011.

Laura Lawson	*City Bountiful: A Century of Community Gardening in America.* Berkeley: University of California Press, 2005.
Darrin Nordahl	*Public Produce: The New Urban Agriculture.* Washington, DC: Island Press, 2009.
Jac Smit, Annu Ratta, and Joe Nasr	*Urban Agriculture: Food, Jobs, and Sustainable Cities.* New York: United Nations Development Programme, 1996.

Film and Video

John Domokos	*Guerrillas Conquer the Elephant.* TheGuardian.com, April 24, 2008. www.theguardian.com/environment /video/2008/apr/25/guerrilla.gardening.
Andrew Hasse, Carl Grether, and Adam Goldstein	*Edible City: Grow the Revolution.* Top Documentary Films, 2012. http://topdocumentaryfilms.com /edible-city-grow-revolution.

Periodicals and Internet Sources

Katherine Alaimo et al.	"Fruit and Vegetable Intake Among Urban Community Gardeners," *Journal of Nutrition Education and Behavior*, vol. 40, no. 2, 2008.
Alison Alkon and Kari Norgaard	"Breaking the Food Chains: An Investigation of Food Justice Activism," *Sociological Inquiry*, vol. 79, no. 3, 2009.

Martin Bailkey   "A Report from New Orleans:
                        Growing Food in a Recovering City,"
                        Urban Agriculture Magazine, no. 21,
                        January 2009. www.ruaf.org.

Sandra Barrera   "The 'Honeybee Underground'
                        Rescues Bees, Promotes Backyard
                        Beekeeping in a Neighborhood Near
                        You," *Los Angeles Daily News*, May
                        19, 2011.

Larry Barszewski   "Backyard Beekeepers Look for
                        Home in South Florida," *Sun
                        Sentinel*, November 24, 2011.
                        http://articles.sun-sentinel.com.

Anne Bellows,   "Health Benefits of Urban
Katherine Brown,   Agriculture," Community Food
and Jac Smit   Security Coalition's North American
                        Initiative on Community Agriculture,
                        2011. www.co.fresno.ca.us.

Alan Bjerga   "Foodies Fight to Save Detroit with
                        Job Hopes Pinned on Arugula,"
                        Bloomberg.com, August 8, 2013.
                        www.bloomberg.com.

Dan Charles   "At the Community Garden, It's
                        Community That's the Hard Part,"
                        National Public Radio, March 20,
                        2012. www.npr.org.

Sena Christian   "A Growing Concern," *Earth Island
                        Journal*, Summer 2010. http://
                        earthisland.org.

Ian Elwood   "Dangers of Urban Farming,"
                          VegNews, January 17, 2012.
                          http://vegnews.com.

Sajid Farooq   "Oakland Sprouting New Farming
                          Laws," NBCBayArea.com, July 22,
                          2011. www.nbcbayarea.com.

Mary Flaherty   "Farm Growth Means More Leafy
                          Greens for Oakland,"
                          Berkeleyside.com, February 4, 2013.
                          www.berkeleyside.com.

Amy Goodman   "Detroit Urban Agriculture
                          Movement Looks to Reclaim Motor
                          City," Democracy Now!, June 24,
                          2010. www.democracynow.org.

Jamie Gross   "That Big Farm Called San
                          Francisco," *New York Times*, April 23,
                          2010.

Stephanie Hanes   "Couple Fined for Having Garden:
                          Take That, Urban Vegetable
                          Gardening Trend," *The Christian
                          Science Monitor*, January 9, 2013.

Jason Helvenston   "Legalize Sustainability: Join Us in
and Jennifer   Our Fight for Food Freedom," *The
Helvenston   Daily Caller*, January 7, 2013.
                          http://dailycaller.com.

Sarah Henry   "Urban Farmer Willow Rosenthal
                          Plants Seeds in Berkeley,"
                          Berkeleyside.com, March 2011.
                          www.berkeleyside.com.

P.J. Huffstutter — "For Backyard-Farmer Companies, Business Is Bountiful," *Los Angeles Times*, May 2, 2010.

Richard Jackson — "The Role of Community Gardens in Sustaining Healthy Communities," Designing Healthy Communities, October 16, 2013. http://designinghealthycommunities.org.

Ryan Jaslow — "Community Gardening Could Carry Health Benefits," CBS News, April 22, 2013. www.cbsnews.com.

Madeleine Key — "City Slicker Farms Breaks Ground on New Urban Park and Farm," *East Bay Express*, January 30, 2013.

Les Kishler — "Community Gardens Are a Serious Answer to Food Supplies," *San Jose Mercury News*, March 18, 2010.

Heather Knight — "Newsom's Fresh Idea: Mandates on Healthy Food," *San Francisco Chronicle*, July 9, 2009.

Lori Kozlowski — "Urban Beekeepers Know It's More than Just Honey and Money," *Los Angeles Times*, March 31, 2009.

Matthai Kuruvila — "Oakland Urban Farming Prompts Plan to Redo Rules," *San Francisco Chronicle*, May 9, 2011.

J.D. McAleese and Linda Rankin "Garden-Based Nutrition Education Affects Fruit and Vegetable Consumption in Sixth-Grade Adolescents," *Journal of the American Dietetic Association*, vol. 107, no. 4, 2007.

Tracie McMillan "Urban Farmers' Crops Go from Vacant Lot to Market," *New York Times*, May 7, 2008.

Meredith Niles "Urban Homesteading in Washington, D.C.," *Grist*, July 16, 2008. http://grist.org.

Erica Reder "West Oakland Group Wins Major Grant for New Urban Farm and Park," *Bay Nature*, November 2010.

Lee Romney "New California Law Aims to Cultivate Urban Agriculture," *Los Angeles Times*, October 2, 2013.

Debby Rubenstein "Back Yard Chickens: STILL Not the Best Hatched Plan," HaveAHeartFarm.org, April 30, 2012. www.haveaheartfarm.org.

Catherine Ryan "Home Is Where the Food Grows," *Terrain*, Winter 2009. http://catherine-ryan.com/wp-content /uploads/2009/12/TERRAIN _HomeIsWhereTheFoodGrows.pdf.

Kristina Shevory "The Beekeeper Next Door," *New York Times*, December 8, 2010.

Everett Sizemore "Backyard Chickens and Bureaucrats: The Regulatory Hurdles for Urban Homesteads," Sustainablog.org, January 18, 2010. http://sustainablog .org.

Rebecca Solnit "Revolutionary Plots," *Orion Magazine*, July–August 2012. www.orionmagazine.org.

S. Swartz et al. "Urban Gardening Yields Benefits for Low Income Families," *Journal of the American Dietetic Association*, vol. 103, no. 9, 2003.

Madeleine Thomas "City Slicker Farms Breaks Ground on New West Oakland Urban Farm," Oakland North, February 2, 2013. http://oaklandnorth.net.

Brad Tuttle "Front Yard Garden Controversy Revelation: Lawns Are Useless," *Time*, July 11, 2011.

Jess Watson "Envisioning Sustainable Futures for Urban Farms," *Edible East Bay*, Spring 2011. http://edibleeastbay.com.

Bobby White "A Garden Grows in Oakland," *Wall Street Journal*, August 26, 2008.

Index